THE TRANSPARENT SELF
Self-Disclosure and Well-Being

by

SIDNEY M. JOURARD
University of Florida

AN INSIGHT BOOK

D. VAN NOSTRAND COMPANY, INC.
PRINCETON, NEW JERSEY
TORONTO   LONDON   MELBOURNE

158
JOT

Van Nostrand Regional Offices:
New York, Chicago, San Francisco

D. Van Nostrand Company, Ltd., London

D. Van Nostrand Company (Canada), Ltd., Toronto

D. Van Nostrand Australia Pty Ltd., Melbourne

PRINTED IN THE UNITED STATES OF AMERICA

Preface

A choice that confronts every one of us at every moment is this: Shall we permit our fellow men to know us as we now *are,* or shall we seek instead to remain an enigma, an uncertain quantity, wishing to be seen as something we are not?

This choice has always been available to us, but throughout history we have chosen to conceal our authentic being behind various masks. We usually assume that the *other* man is hiding or misrepresenting his real feelings, his intentions, or his past because we generally do so ourselves. We take it for granted that when a man speaks about himself, he is telling more or less than the unvarnished truth as he knows it.

We conceal and camouflage our true being before others to foster a sense of safety, to protect ourselves against unwanted but expected criticism, hurt, or rejection. This protection is purchased at a steep price. When we are not truly known by the other people in our lives, we are misunderstood. When we are not known, even by family and friends, we join the all too numerous "lonely crowd." Worse, when we succeed too well in hiding our being from others, we tend to lose touch with our real selves, and this loss of self contributes to illness in its myriad forms.

The curious thing to me, as a psychologist, is that we have not seriously questioned man's *decision* to hide rather than to reveal himself. Indeed, self-concealment is regarded as the most natural state for grown men. People who reveal themselves in simple honesty are sometimes seen as childish, crazy, or naïve, as for example, in Dostoievsky's novel *The Idiot,* or Melville's *Billy Budd.* The uncritical assumption that concealment is the natural state for man, more natural than candor, has given rise to many stratagems for getting inside a man's defenses and pretensions. The stratagems run the gamut from attempting to get a man drunk to asking him to report his dreams or to indicate what he sees in some inkblots. Here, the assumption is that he will then, in spite of himself, give hints of what he has been hiding.

Yet, recent experience and research is beginning to show that such methods of getting to know a person or getting him to "open up" are unnecessary when a man *wants* to be known. Under these conditions, he will do everything in his power to make sure that the other person's image of him is as accurate as possible. He will show the same concern to be known that a less honest person will to assure that the other individual has a false picture of him.

I became fascinated with the phenomenon of self-disclosure after puzzling about the fact that patients who consulted me for therapy told me more about themselves than they had ever told another living person. Many of them said, "You are the first person I have ever been completely honest with." I wondered whether there was some connection between their reluctance to be known by spouse, family, and friends and their need to consult with a professional psychotherapist. My fascination with self-disclosure led me on a conceptual and empirical odyssey, some aspects of which are described in the chapters that follow.

Another phenomenon, not completely separable from self-disclosure, is what I have called "spirit." There is increasing scientific evidence that man's physical and psychological health are profoundly affected by the degree to which he has found meaning, direction, and purpose in his existence. Some at least of this purpose and meaning arises in man's relationships with his fellows. I suspect that a man's life begins to lose in meaning most rapidly when he becomes estranged from his fellows, when they become strangers to him and when he lets himself become a stranger to them; when he distrusts others so much he misleads them into thinking they know him when, in fact, he knows that they do not and cannot. "Spirit" is a term which scientists view with a certain suspicion, as a matter which does not lend itself to scientific study. I acknowledge the legitimacy of this reluctance to study the phenomena of "spirit," yet there is more to man than the structures and drives he shares with animals. Consequently, I have taken a fresh look at whatever there is that can be seen when the layman or poet speaks of spirit, and I have attempted to bring these phenomena within the scope of scientific analysis. Part of this book shows the result of my thinking in this area. It is my hope that investigators of human motivation will find some stimulation there to seek better ways to measure spirit, or levels of "inspiritation," thereby fostering further research into this important area.

The book as a whole expresses the hypothesis that man can attain to health and fuller functioning only insofar as he gains in courage to be himself among others and when he finds goals and objectives that have value and meaning for him. I would like this book to be read by research psychologists, counselors and psychotherapists, ministers, nurses, and health scientists as well as by students of mental health. And, of course, I welcome the attention of interested laymen who wish to become acquainted with some recent thinking in a field that touches upon their potential for fuller functioning as human beings.

SIDNEY M. JOURARD

Gainesville, Florida

Contents

PART V. A NEW WAY OF BEING FOR NURSES

A TECHNICAL APPENDIX FOR PSYCHOLOGISTS

1

Introduction:
Self-Disclosure and the Mystery
of the Other Man*

If I look naïvely at my fellow man, I see him doing all
manner of things, and I have no way of predicting or
understanding why he does what he does. In fact, I may
fear him, as I fear anything which acts with caprice. I
may impute motives like mine to him, as primitive man
imputed human motives to animals, the sea, plants, and
the weather. I may engage in magic, ritual, or other super-
stitious practices, as primitive men did, in order to get
others to help me or leave me alone.

But when man learned the conditions which were responsible for the behavior of the weather, the sea, plants,
and animals, he feared them less and became more able
to enlist their collaboration for the pursuit of his ends.
He no longer imputed characteristics to these things
which they did not possess, but strove, rather, to ascertain
their real characteristics and to understand the forces
which moved them. Man's fear changed then to respect.

With his fellow, however, man continues to behave
much as he did in earlier times with plants, animals, and
elements. His concepts and beliefs about the other man
are usually based on insufficient or emotionally distorted
evidence, and they are thus often false. Consequently, a
man may find himself living in a world of strangers whose
actions are either misunderstood or misinterpreted. And
he becomes afraid.

The other man is a mystery. He is opaque. We cannot
know in advance what he will do. We do not know his
past, and we do not know what is "going on inside him."

* Prepared for the series, "Conversations Between Psychology and Theology," Presbyterian Student Center, University of
Florida, April 3, 1959.

1

Consequently, we remain on guard when we are in his presence. Naïve observation will show that the other man behaves predictably some of the time in the ritual of social living. He clothes himself, goes to work, tips his hat to ladies, utters polite conversation, and in short, seems "normal"—unless he is a foreigner, a psychotic, or a child. In the latter instances, we may be frank in admitting we don't know what he is thinking, and even if he tells us, we may not understand because we don't know his language. Or, erroneously, we may assume that we know his motives, thoughts, and reactions. But even with "normal" people, most of us feel rather uneasy, because we do not always know what they are thinking. In fact, if "normal" people tell us what they are thinking, what they feel, believe, or day-dream about, many of us feel, with a certain un-ease, that we are being "snowed" —the man isn't leveling with us. He is telling us what he thinks we want to hear. Often, he is doing just that. Because he may mislead us in telling us what he is like, we become shocked when we read that Mr. Jones, without warning, took a hatchet and butchered his family, whom he seemed to love so well.

> "Things are seldom what they seem,
> Skim milk masquerades as cream."

> "Externals don't portray insides,
> Jekylls may be masking Hydes."

Let me apologize for such atrocious verse and then point up an empirical fact. Man, perhaps alone of all living forms, is capable of *being* one thing and *seeming* from his actions and talk to be something else. Not even those animals and insects and fishes which Nature expertly camouflages can do this "seeming" at will; they do it reflexly.

Now, let me mention another truism. If Mr. Jones, the one who butchered his family, had *frankly* disclosed his inner thoughts, feelings, and plans to you, then news of his butchery would have come to you as no surprise. You would have understood it. Perhaps you could have predicted it and then interfered, thus saving the lives of his "loved ones."

It is a simple, patent fact that when a man discloses his self, his inner experience to another, fully, spontaneously, and honestly, then the mystery that he was decreases enormously. When a man discloses himself to me, I find all my preconceptions and beliefs about him becoming altered, one after the other, by the facts as they come forth—unless, of course, I have a vested interest in continuing to believe untruths about him.

In the general scheme of things, what consequences follow when men disclose their real selves one to the other? Here are some of the more obvious outcomes:

—They learn the extent to which they are similar one to the other, and the extent to which they differ from one another in thoughts, feelings, hopes, reactions to the past, etc.

—They learn of the other man's needs, enabling them to help him meet them or else to ensure that they will not be met.

—They learn the extent to which this man accords with or deviates from moral and ethical standards for being and behaving. Here we may have a reason why people are reluctant to disclose themselves: they dread the moral judgment of their friends, family, minister, or the law.

I don't want to belabor the point, but I think it is almost self-evident that you cannot love another person, that is, behave toward him so as to foster his happiness and growth, unless you know what he needs. And you cannot know what he needs unless he tells you.

You cannot collaborate with another person toward some common end unless you know him. How can you know him, and he you, unless you have engaged in enough mutual disclosure of self to be able to anticipate how he will react and what part he will play?

Why do we disclose ourselves, and why do we not? Answers to this question are of enormous importance, since ignorance between man and man seems to be partly at the root of just about all current world problems. We do not know the Russians, for example, though I suspect we have disclosed ourselves much more to them than vice-versa; furthermore, through an effective spy service, they have learned much about us that we would not freely disclose. Possibly, the Russian leaders want to prevent us from disclosing ourselves fully to the Russian people because they fear that such disclosure will show the Russian man-in-the-street that we have much in common with him regarding life's goals. But we have often tried to block teachers' disclosures of what they know and think about Russian life, political system, etc., because we *want* young people to have prejudiced concepts of "the Russian."

Researches that I have been undertaking point strongly to the likelihood that a person will disclose himself, permit himself to be known, only when he believes that his audience is a man of good will. To put this another way, self-disclosure follows an attitude of love and trust. If I love someone, not only do I strive to know him, so that I can devote myself more effectively to his well-being; *I also display my love by letting him know me*. At the same time, by so doing, I permit him to love me.

But loving is a scary business because when you permit yourself to be known you expose yourself, not only to a lover's balm, but also to a hater's bombs! When he knows you, he knows just where to plant them for maximum effect.

In a poker game, no man discloses the content of his hand to the other players. Instead, he tries to dissemble and bluff. If he holds four aces, he tries to get the others to believe his hand is empty, until it is time for the showdown. If he holds nothing, he tries to seem as if he holds four aces in order to get something for nothing. In a society which pits man against man, as in a poker game, people do keep a poker face; they wear a mask and let no one know what they are up to. In a society where man is *for* man, then the psychological iron curtain is dropped.

But now a paradox, turned up through research. Surely within the family, where love is expected to prevail, and people will *be* themselves, we find much evidence for dissembling, for the lack of mutual disclosure. Children do not know their parents; fathers do not know what their children think, or what they are doing. Husbands and wives often are strangers one to the other to an incredible degree.

We are said to be a society dedicated, among other things, to the pursuit of truth. Yet, disclosure of the truth, the truth of one's being, is often penalized. Impossible concepts of how man ought to be—which, sadly enough are often handed down from the pulpit—make man so ashamed of his true being that he feels obliged to seem different, if for no other reason than to protect his job. Probably the "tyranny of the should" is a factor which keeps man from making himself known as he is. Yet, when a man does not acknowledge to himself who, what, and how he is, he is out of touch with reality, and he will sicken and die; and no one can help him without access to the facts. And it seems to be another empirical fact that *no man can come to know himself except as an outcome of disclosing himself to another person.* This is the lesson we have learned in the field of psychotherapy. When a person has been able to disclose himself utterly to another person, he learns how to increase his contact with his real self, and he may then be better able to direct his destiny on the basis of knowledge of his real self.

But outside the clinic, disclosure of man to man, honest, direct, uncontrived, is the necessary condition for reducing the mystery that one man is for another. It is the empirical index of an I-Thou relationship, which I, agreeing with Buber (1937), see as the index of man functioning at his highest and truly *human* level rather than at the level of a thing or animal. It is the means by which people become able to collaborate or else to learn that in reality they are far too different one from the other to collaborate in this particular enterprise. Disclosure of man to man appears to be the most direct means by which we can all learn wherein we are identical with our fellow man and wherein we differ. Such knowledge, suitably evaluated, then provides us with the basis for action which can either destroy man or meet his needs for more abundant and human living. Self-disclosure, my communication of my private world to you, in language which you clearly understand, is truly an important bit of behavior for us to learn something about. You can know me truly only if I let you, only if I *want* you to know me. Your misunderstanding of me is only partly your fault. If I want you to know me, I shall find a means of communicating myself to you. If you want me to reveal myself, just demonstrate your good will—your will to employ your powers for my good, and not for my destruction.

Part I

Self-Disclosure as a Psychological Fact

2

Self-Disclosure: The Scientist's Portal to Man's Soul

The soul of which poets speak, and which philosophers and theologians concern themselves with, is now operationally defined by psychologists and called the Self. That the soul, or self, is real, in the sense of existing, few can doubt. At least few would doubt its reality when we define the self as the subjective side of man—that which is private and personal, which he experiences immediately and spontaneously. Of course, what we term "self" has correlates—neurophysiological correlates and environmental stimuli. Doubtless too, the self—feelings, wishes, memories, thoughts, dreams, etc.—is lawful as well. But the self is unique in all of nature, though it is a part of nature. It is unique in this respect: Any other part of nature passively submits to the inquiry of the investigator who is after the facts. Man's self, as near as we now know, can never be known to any save the experiencing individual unless the individual man unequivocably co-operates and *makes his self known*. In short, man must consent; if we would know his self, he must *want* to tell us. If he doesn't wish to tell us of his self, we can torture him, browbeat him, tempt him, even make incisive psychoanalytic guesses; but unless he wishes to make his self known, we will of course never know it. However shrewd our guesses might be about a man's self, when we guess about a man's self, we never know whether we are correct until he says, and means it, "You're right." Moreover, we don't know for a certainty whether he means it.

This line of thinking should make us despair of ever subjecting man's soul to scientific scrutiny, except for one thing. It is likely that the *act* of self-disclosure follows laws—perhaps the laws of reinforcement (cf. Skinner, 1953). I believe that I may have stumbled upon a key to

the lock of the portal to man's soul. So far, the key barely
fits the lock; it doesn't always work; it needs to be made
more precise, of course. But it is such an obvious kind of
key, and it has been lying around unnoticed for such a
long time, that I wonder why no one ever picked it up to
try it out for size.

What is this key? It is the study of what information a
person will tell another person about himself, or, more
technically, about his *self*. I call the key—or portal, it
doesn't really matter, since we are mixing metaphors—
self-disclosure. Through my self-disclosure, I let others
know my soul. They can know it, really know it, only as I
make it known. In fact, I am beginning to suspect that
I can't even know *my own soul* except as I disclose it.
I suspect that I will know myself "for real" at the exact
moment that I have succeeded in making it known
through my disclosure to another person.

Let us look for a moment at the act of disclosing something about one's self to another person, a simple statement such as one's name, age, weight, height, what one
did with whom yesterday, or the relating of a dream. A
little introspection will verify that even simple, factual
disclosures of this sort can often be matters that are
fraught with anxiety. Whence the anxiety? Cameron and
Magaret (1951) have a section in their excellent treatise
on *Behavior Pathology* which is concerned with what they
call behavioral duplicity. They point out that dissemblance is learned early in life by all of us. As children we
are, and we *act*, our real selves. We say what we think,
we scream for what we want, we tell what we did. These
spontaneous disclosures meet variable consequences—
some disclosures are ignored, some rewarded, and some
punished. Doubtless in accordance with the laws of reinforcement, we learn early to withhold certain disclosures because of the painful consequences to which
they lead. We are punished, in our society, not only for
what we actually do, but also for what we think, feel, or
want. Very soon, then, the growing child learns to display a highly expurgated version of his self to others. I
have coined the term "public self" (Jourard, 1958) to
refer to the concept of oneself which one *wants* others to
believe. We monitor, censor our behavior and disclosures

in order to construct in the mind of the other person a concept of ourselves which we want him to have. Obviously, our assorted public selves are not always accurate portrayals of our real selves. In fact, it often comes to pass—perhaps as a socially patterned defect (Fromm, 1955)—that our public selves become so estranged from our real selves that the net consequence is self-alienation: we no longer know our real selves. Our disclosures reflect, not our spontaneous feelings, thoughts, and wishes, but rather pretended experience which will avoid punishment and win unearned approval. We say that we feel things we do not feel. We say that we did things we did not do. We say that we believe things we do not believe. When self-alienation, which I believe is the consequence of what I call pseudo-self-disclosure, has proceeded far enough, the individual loses his soul, literally. Or, we may say he has sold his soul, his real self, in order to purchase popularity, his mother's affection, or a promotion in the firm.

Self-disclosure, then, entails courage—the kind of courage that Paul Tillich (1952) had in mind in writing his book *The Courage to Be*. I would paraphrase that title to read, *The Courage to Be Known*, since Being always occurs in a social context. Since I seem to be in a paraphrasing frame of mind, let me modify some other well-known sayings. The Delphic Oracle advised, "Know Thyself"; I would say "Make Thyself Known, and then Thou wilt Know Thyself." Shakespeare is the source of, "And this above all, to thine own self be true, and . . . thou cans't not then be false to any man." Let me re-state it, "And this above all, to any other man be true, and thou cans't not then be false to thyself."

What, after all, is the situation called psychotherapy, but a situation wherein one person, the patient—alienated from himself, troubled—starts to disclose his self to the other person, the therapist. Then he "blocks," he resists. The therapist uses his skill to overcome the resistance, thus promoting more self-disclosure. Whether or not psychotherapy works as well as nothing or anything, as Eysenck (1952) seems to believe (I do not really believe he really believes this), of one thing we can be sure: At the conclusion of a series of psychotherapeutic sessions, the therapist knows more about his patient's self than he knew at the beginning. Possibly, too, the patient knows more about his own self at that time too. What he does with this knowledge is of course another cup of tea.

Does it come as a shock that, in the studies conducted at Chicago by Rogers (1954) into the effects of psychotherapy, that after umpteen hours of therapy, the therapist could guess the self-description of his patient better than he could at the outset of therapy? It is a case of the therapist being taught by the patient's self-disclosures of what manner of a man the patient believes he is. Should we assert that empathy is facilitated by self-disclosure? Let's ask the question, "How do we obtain an accurate concept of another man's experiencing?" We can guess his experience on the basis of interpretations of such things as facial cues; we can indulge in assimilative projection, imagine how we would feel in that situation, and then assume that that in fact is what the other man *is* at the moment. A more effective way of obtaining an accurate concept of the man's experiencing is to ask him what he is thinking and feeling. If he tells us honestly, there we have it: the basis for perfect empathy.

I could go on in this vein, but I had better not. I have some data that I would like to share with you. Let me tell you of a method we have been using to study self-disclosure, and some findings. Then, I shall conclude with some plans, or rather hopes that I have for further investigation.

A few years ago, I was puzzling about Karen Horney's (1950) concept of the "real self." I wondered how to adapt this concept for purposes of research. Out of this thinking came the idea that the kind of personal data we all put down on an application form when we are applying for a job might have the makings of a research tool. Some application forms, labeled "confidential," ask for amazingly detailed data about oneself. I asked myself, "Whom would an applicant tell these things to besides his prospective employer, or teacher?" And then I was off. I started itemizing classes of information about oneself which could only be known by another person through direct verbal telling. After much fiddling this way and that, I wound up with a 60-item questionnaire (see Appendix I) listing 10 items of information in each of 6 categories, which I called Aspects of Self. I devised an answer sheet with rows corresponding to the items, and columns headed by Target-Persons. To start with, I arbitrarily selected Mother, Father, Male Friend, and Female Friend and/or Spouse as Target-Persons. Subjects were asked to indicate whether or not they had made information about each item known to each of the Target-Persons. Those devotees of analysis of variance can see the makings of a colossal pot of data to be unscrambled with that method. After all, we had four or five Target-Persons and six Aspects of Self; our subjects could be classified endlessly (male-female, Negro-white, good-bad, etc.); and not the least, we had individual differences to look into.

My colleague Paul Lasakow and I tested several hundred subjects with this simple instrument, and we selected smaller subsamples for particular analyses. Here are some of the things that we found. Men do not disclose as much about themselves, generally, as women. White subjects of both sexes disclose more, generally, than Negro subjects of comparable social class and educational level. For the age range we studied: white females disclose most to mother and girl friend, and least to father and boy friend; Negro females follow a similar pattern. White males disclose in about equivalent amount to both parents and male friend, and significantly less to female friend. Negro males disclose most to their mothers, and comparatively little, if at all, to father, male friend, or female friend.

Married subjects, of course, disclose most to their spouse. With regard to other target-persons, such as both parents, and the same-sex friend, female married subjects disclose more than male married subjects, though there is no sex difference in disclosure to the spouse. I am led to suspect that males are relatively unknown to and by anyone until they marry, while women are better known. In fact, it seems that women are both the givers and the receivers of subjective data. Women know more, and tell more, about people's selves than men do. This, doubtless, is part of their "expressive role" in social systems, in contrast with the male "instrumental role." It staggers me a little when I think of the stupendous amount of private and personal "self-data" that women have at their disposal. Men know the facts of nature, but women know the facts about men and women!

In connection with the theme of marriage, we are led, of course, to love. Married subjects, male and female, disclose less to their parents and friends than unmarried subjects of comparable age. What they have taken away from these folks, in the way of self-disclosure, they give unto their spouses. In this respect, they more or less follow the biblical injunction which holds that in marriage one should forsake all others. However, while our young married females obeyed the spirit of this injunction, they did not obey its letter—Momma was still disclosed to quite a bit by these young wives. Presumably, there is love in marriage. The loved spouse is disclosed to more than other target-persons. But we have more direct data than this, concerned with the relation between love and self-disclosure. Questionnaires measuring the feelings of a group of young female subjects toward their mothers and fathers produced scores that correlated substantially with self-disclosure to mother and father. In other words, when one loves or likes one's parents, one will make oneself known to them; not otherwise. Of course, psychotherapists are familiar with this fact; self-disclosure gets dammed up in their patients with every twinge of negative transference. And it is influenced by both positive and negative *counter*transference. But I am led to propose that when poets speak of love as a case of giving one's heart and soul to another, they are speaking, among other things, of this prosaic thing, self-disclosure.

Here is an interesting finding. Married police officers were compared with young married college males on self-disclosure to Wife and to Closest Male Friend. Compared with the college boys, the police officers were tight-lipped. Their wives and friends knew virtually nothing about them. Is this paranoia? An occupational pattern?

I am beginning to formulate a rather crude hypothesis about self-disclosure, one which is strongly suggested by certain patterns in our data. Let me state it rather dogmatically, so that it can be more readily tested. Speaking generally, we see in our data that our subjects disclose more to their family than to non-family members, and excepting the married subjects, more to their own sex than to the opposite sex; and they disclose more to their age-peers than to their elders or youngers. In other words, the subjects tended to disclose more about themselves to people who *resembled them in various ways* than to people who differed from them. This leads me to propose that disclosure of self is a byproduct, among other things, of the perception or belief that the other, the target-person, is similar to the self. Probably the similarity which is crucial is similarity in *values*. We disclose ourselves when we are pretty sure that the target-person will evaluate our disclosures and react to them as we do ourselves (within certain limits).

Another finding of a general nature is obvious and was expected. The aspects of self were differentially disclosed. Obviously, some kinds of information about ourselves are easier to disclose than others. Psychotherapists are familiar with this fact, as were Kurt Lewin (1948) and, more recently, Maria Rickers-Ovsiankina (1956).

Where to follow this self-disclosure next? There are many avenues, not the least in importance being efforts to refine our instrument, which at present is very crude. But we can explore many general hypotheses in a broad spade-work operation—age-changes, social class, many and many group comparisons. We can explore content systematically for its varying ease of disclosure. We can investigate, even map, interpersonal relationships, lending a depth dimension to sociometry. I'm of course interested in the mental health implications of self-disclosure.

Let me comment a little about self-disclosure and mental health. I really don't know which is cause and which is effect here; perhaps it doesn't matter. I have some evidence that the relationship between the two variables is curvilinear—too much or too little self-disclosure betokens disturbance in self and in interpersonal relationships, while some as yet undetermined amount under specified conditions is synonymous with mental health. I believe that self-disclosure is the obverse of repression and self-alienation. The man who is alienated from his fellows is alienated from himself. Alienated man is not known by his fellows, he doesn't know himself, and he doesn't know his fellows. Self-disclosure appears to be one means, perhaps the most direct, by which self-alienation is transformed into self-realization. Man hides much of his real self—his experience—behind an iron curtain. Our evidence shows that this iron curtain melts like wax when it is exposed to the warm breath of love.

I will conclude by sharing with you some less scientific aspects of the study of self-disclosure. Another man's self is an utterly fascinating datum. We spend much of our time in our daily life speculating about the other person's self; we have to in order to interact with him. Our purposes in securing knowledge of the other man's self vary, of course, but it is not difficult to see how one could become a student of others' selves for the love of the game. If I seem repetitious, enthusiastic, or both, I am like the guitar-player who, daily, for 20 years, sat with a one-string guitar, holding the same fret, plucking the same sound. One day his wife said, with surprise, "Dear, I noticed on TV today that a man was playing a guitar, but it had six strings, and the man kept moving his hands around, and making lots of different sounds—not like you." Her husband said, "Don't worry about him, dear. He's still huntin' the right note, and I already found it."

Part II

The Importance of Self-Disclosure
in Human Experience

3

Healthy Personality
and Self-Disclosure*

For a long time, health and well-being have been taken for granted as "givens," and disease has been viewed as the problem for man to solve. Today, however, increasing numbers of scientists have begun to adopt a reverse point of view: disease and trouble are coming to be viewed as the givens, and specification of positive health and its conditions as the important goal. Physical, mental, and social health are values representing restrictions on the total variance of being. The scientific problem here consists in arriving at a definition of health, determining its relevant dimensions, and then identifying the independent variables of which these are a function.

Scientists, however, are supposed to be hard-boiled, and they insist that phenomena, in order to be counted "real," must be public. Hence, many behavioral scientists ignore man's self, or soul, since it is essentially a private phenomenon. Others, however, are not so quick to allocate man's self to the limbo of the unimportant, and they insist that we cannot understand man and his lot until we take his self into account.

I probably fall into the camp of these investigators who want to explore health as a positive problem in its own right and who, further, take man's self seriously—as a reality to be explained and as a variable which produces consequences for weal or woe. In this chapter, I would like more fully to explore the connection between positive health and the disclosure of self. Let me commence with some sociological truisms.

Social systems require their members to play certain

* Talk given November 20, 1958, at a meeting of the North Florida Section of the American Personnel and Guidance Association and published in *Mental Hygiene*, Vol. 43, 1959.

roles. Unless the roles are adequately played, the social systems will not produce the results for which they have been organized. This flat statement applies to social systems as simple as one developed by an engaged couple and to those as complex as a total nation among nations.

Societies have socialization "factories" and "mills"—families and schools—which serve the function of training people to play the age, sex, and occupational roles which they shall be obliged to play throughout their life in the social system. Broadly speaking, if a person plays his roles suitably, he can be regarded as a more or less normal personality. *Normal personalities, however, are not necessarily healthy personalities* (Jourard, 1958, pp. 16-18).

Healthy personalities are people who play their roles satisfactorily and at the same time derive personal satisfaction from role enactment; more, they keep growing and they maintain high-level physical wellness (Dunn, 1958). It is probably enough, speaking from the standpoint of a stable social system, for people to be normal personalities. But it is possible to be a normal personality and be absolutely miserable. We would count such a normal personality unhealthy. In fact, normality in some social systems—successful acculturation to them—reliably produces ulcers, piles, paranoia, or compulsiveness. We also have to regard as unhealthy those people who have never been able to enact the roles that legitimately can be expected from them.

Counselors, guidance workers, and psychotherapists are obliged to treat with both patterns of unhealthy personality—those people who have been unable to learn their roles and those who play their roles quite well, but suffer the agonies of boredom, frustration, anxiety, or stultification. If our clients are to be helped, they must change, and change in *valued* directions. A change in a valued direction may arbitrarily be called growth. We have yet to give explicit statement to these valued directions for growth, though a beginning has been made (Fromm, 1947; Jahoda, 1958; Jourard, 1958; Maslow, 1954; Rogers, 1954). We who are professionally concerned with the happiness, growth, and well-being of our clients may be regarded as professional lovers, not unlike the Cyprian sisterhood. It would be fascinating to pursue this parallel further, but for the moment let us ask instead what this has to do with self-disclosure.

To answer this question, let's tune in on an imaginary interview between a client and his counselor. The client says, "I have never told this to a soul, doctor, but I can't stand my wife, my mother is a nag, my father is a bore, and my boss is an absolutely hateful and despicable tyrant. I have been carrying on an affair for the past ten years with the lady next door, and at the same time I am a deacon in the church." The counselor says, showing great understanding and empathy, "Mm-humm!"

If we listened for a long enough period of time, we would find that the client talks and talks about himself to this highly sympathetic and empathic listener. At some later time, the client may eventually say, "Gosh, you have helped me a lot. I see what I must do and I will go ahead and do it."

Now this talking about oneself to another person is what I call self-disclosure. It would appear, without assuming anything, that self-disclosure is a factor in the process of effective counseling or psychotherapy. Would it be too arbitrary an assumption to propose that people become clients *because they have not disclosed themselves in some optimum degree to the people in their life?*

An historical digression: Toward the end of the 19th century, Joseph Breuer, a Viennese physician, discovered (probably accidentally) that when his hysterical patients talked about themselves, disclosing not only the verbal content of their memories, but also the feelings that they had suppressed at the time of assorted "traumatic" experiences, their hysterical symptoms disappeared. Somewhere along the line, Breuer withdrew from a situation which would have made him Freud's peer in history's hall of fame. When Breuer permitted his patients "to be," it scared him, one gathers, because some of his female patients disclosed themselves to be quite sexy, and what was probably worse, they felt quite sexy toward him. Freud, however, did not flinch. He made the momentous discovery that the neurotic people of his time were struggling like mad to avoid "being," to avoid being known, and in Allport's (1955) terms, to avoid "be-coming." He learned that his patients, when they were given the opportunity to "be"—which free association on a couch is nicely designed to do—would disclose that they had all manner of horrendous thoughts and feelings which they did not even dare disclose to themselves, much less express in the presence of another person. Freud learned to permit his patients to be, through per-mitting them to disclose themselves utterly to another human. He evidently did not trust anyone enough to be willing to disclose himself *vis à vis*, so he disclosed him-self to himself on paper (Freud, 1955) and learned the extent to which he was himself self-alienated. Roles for people in Victorian days were even more restrictive than today, and Freud discovered that when people struggled to avoid being and knowing themselves, they got sick. They could only become well and stay relatively well when they came to know themselves through self-disclo-sure to another person. This makes me think of Georg Groddeck's magnificent *Book of the It* (*Id*) in which, in the guise of letters to a naïve young woman, Grod-deck shows the contrast between the *public self*—preten-tious role-playing—and the warded off but highly dy-namic *id*—which I here very loosely translate as "real self."

Let me at this point draw a distinction between role relationships and interpersonal relationships—a distinc-tion which is often overlooked in the current spate of literature that has to do with human relations. Roles are inescapable. They must be played or else the social sys-tem will not work. A role by definition is a repertoire of behavior patterns which must be rattled off in appro-priate contexts, and all behavior which is irrelevant to the role must be suppressed. But what we often forget is the fact that it is a *person* who is playing the role. This person has a self, or I should say he *is* a self. All too often the roles that a person plays do not do justice to all of his self. In fact, there may be nowhere that he may just *be* himself. Even more, the person may not *know* his self. He may, in Horney's (1950) terms, be self-alienated. This fascinating term "self-alienation" means that an individual is estranged from his real self.

His real self becomes a stranger, a feared and distrusted stranger. Estrangement, alienation from one's real self, is at the root of the "neurotic personality of our time" so eloquently described by Horney (1936). Fromm (1957) referred to the same phenomenon as a socially patterned defect. Self-alienation is a sickness which is so widely shared that no one recognizes it. We may take it for granted that all the clients whom we encounter are self-alienated to a greater or lesser extent. If you ask anyone to answer the question, "Who are you?" the answer will generally be "I am a psychologist," "a businessman," a "teacher," or what have you. The respondent will probably tell you the name of the role with which he feels most closely identified. As a matter of fact, the respondent spends a great part of his life trying to discover who he is, and once he has made some such discovery, he spends the rest of his life trying to play the part. Of course, some of the roles—age, sex, family, or occupational roles —may be so restrictive that they fit a person in a manner not too different from the girdle of a 200-pound lady who is struggling to look like Brigitte Bardot. There is Faustian drama all about us in this world of role-playing. Everywhere we see people who have sold their soul, or their real self, if you wish, in order to be a psychologist, a businessman, a nurse, a physician, a this or a that.

Now, I have suggested that no social system can exist unless the members play their roles and play them with precision and elegance. But here is an odd observation, and yet one which you can all corroborate just by thinking back over your own experience. It is possible to be involved in a social group such as a family or a work setting for years and years, playing one's roles nicely with the other members—and never getting to know the *persons* who are playing the other roles. Roles can be played personally and impersonally, as we are beginning to discover. A husband can be married to his wife for fifteen years and never come to know her. He knows her as "the wife." This is the paradox of the "*lonely* crowd" (Riesman, 1950). It is the loneliness which people try to counter with "togetherness." But much of today's "togetherness" is like the "parallel play" of two-year-old

children, or like the professors in Stringfellow Barr's
(1958) novel who, when together socially, lecture *past*
one another alternately and sometimes simultaneously.
There is no real self-to-self or person-to-person meeting
in such transactions. Now what does it mean to know a
person, or, more accurately, a person's self? I don't mean
anything mysterious by "self." All I mean is the person's
subjective side—what he thinks, feels, believes, wants,
worries about—the kind of thing which one could never
know unless one were told. *We get to know the other
person's self when he discloses it to us.*

Self-disclosure, letting another person know what you
think, feel, or want is the most direct means (though
not the only means) by which an individual can make
himself known to another person. Personality hygienists
place great emphasis upon the importance for mental
health of what they call "real-self being," "self-realization," "discovering oneself," and so on. An operational
analysis of what goes on in counseling and therapy
shows that the patients and clients discover themselves
through self-disclosure to the counselor. They talk and,
to their shock and amazement, the counselor listens.

I venture to say that there is probably no experience
more horrifying and terrifying than that of self-disclosure
to "significant others" whose probable reactions are assumed, but not known. Hence the phenomenon of "resistance." This is what makes psychotherapy so difficult
to take, and so difficult to administer. If there is any
skill to be learned in the art of counseling and psychotherapy, it is the art of coping with the terrors which
attend self-disclosure, and the art of decoding the language, verbal and non-verbal, in which a person speaks
about his inner experience.

Now what is the connection between self-disclosure
and healthy personality? Self-disclosure, or should I say
"real"-self-disclosure, is both a symptom of personality
health (Jourard, 1958, pp. 218-221) and at the same
time a means of ultimately achieving healthy personality.
The discloser of self is an animated "real-self be-er."
This, of course, takes courage—the "courage to be." I
have known people who would rather die than become
known. In fact, some did die when it appeared that the

chances were great that they would become known. When I say that self-disclosure is a symptom of personality health, what I mean really is that a person who displays many of the other characteristics that betoken healthy personality (Jourard, 1958; Maslow, 1954) *will also display the ability to make himself fully known to at least one other significant human being.* When I say that self-disclosure is a means by which one achieves personality health, I mean something like the following: it is not until I *am* my real self and I act my real self that my real self is in a position to grow. One's self grows from the *consequence of being.* People's selves stop growing when they repress them. This growth-arrest in the self is what helps to account for the surprising paradox of finding an infant inside the skin of someone who is playing the role of an adult. In a fascinating analysis of mental disease, Jurgen Ruesch (1957) describes assorted neurotics, psychotics, and psychosomatic patients as persons with selective atrophy and overspecialization in various aspects of the process of communication. This culminates in a foul-up of the processes of knowing others and of becoming known to others. Neurotic and psychotic symptoms might be viewed as smoke screens interposed between the patient's real self and the gaze of the onlooker. We might call the symptoms "devices to avoid becoming known." A new theory of schizophrenia has been proposed by a former patient (Anonymous, 1958) who "was there," and he makes such a point.

Alienation from one's real self not only arrests one's growth as a person; it also tends to make a farce out of one's relationships with people. As the ex-patient mentioned above observed, the crucial "break" in schizophrenia is with *sincerity,* not reality (Anonymous, 1958). A self-alienated person—one who does not disclose himself truthfully and fully—can never love another person nor can he be loved by the other person. Effective loving calls for knowledge of the object (Fromm, 1956; Jourard, 1958). How can I love a person whom I do not know? How can the other person love me if he does not know me?

Hans Selye (1946) proposed and documented the hypothesis that illness as we know it arises in consequence of stress applied to the organism. Now I rather think that unhealthy *personality* has a similar root cause, and one which is related to Selye's concept of stress. It is this. Every maladjusted person is a person who has not made himself known to another human being and in consequence does not know himself. Nor can he be himself. More than that, *he struggles actively to avoid becoming known by another human being.* He works at it ceaselessly, 24 hours daily, and it is work! The fact that resisting becoming known is *work* offers us a research opening, incidentally (cf. Dittes, 1958; Davis and Malmo, 1951). I believe that in the effort to avoid becoming known, a person provides for himself a cancerous kind of stress which is subtle and unrecognized but none the less effective in producing, not only the assorted patterns of unhealthy personality which psychiatry talks about, but also the wide array of physical ills that have come to be recognized as the stock in trade of psychosomatic medicine. Stated another way, I believe that *other people come to be stressors to an individual in direct proportion to his degree of self-alienation.*

If I am struggling to avoid becoming known by other persons then, of course, I must construct a false public self (Jourard, 1958, pp. 301-302). The greater the discrepancy between my unexpurgated real self and the version of myself that I present to others, then the more dangerous will other people be for me. If becoming known by another person is threatening, then the very presence of another person can serve as a stimulus to evoke anxiety, heightened muscle tension, and all the assorted visceral changes which occur when a person is under stress. A beginning already has been made, demonstrating the tension-evoking powers of the other person, through the use of such instruments as are employed in the lie detector, through the measurement of muscle tensions with electromyographic apparatus, and so on (Davis and Malmo, 1958; Dittes, 1958).

Students of psychosomatic medicine have been intimating something of what I have just finished saying explicitly. They say (cf. Alexander, 1950) the ulcer patients, asthmatic patients, patients suffering from colitis, migraine, and the like, are chronic *repressors* of certain needs and emotions, especially hostility and dependency. Now when you repress something, you are not only withholding awareness of this something from yourself, you are also withholding it from the scrutiny of the other person. In fact, the means by which repressions are overcome in the therapeutic situation is through relentless disclosure of self to the therapist. When a patient is finally able to follow the fundamental rule in psychoanalysis and disclose everything which passes through his mind, he is generally shocked and dismayed to observe the breadth, depth, range, and diversity of thoughts, memories, and emotions which pass out of his "unconscious" into overt disclosure. Incidentally, by the time a person is that free to disclose in the presence of another human being, he has doubtless completed much of his therapeutic sequence.

Self-disclosure, then, appears to be one of the means by which a person engages in that elegant activity which we call real-self-being. But is real-self-being synonomous with healthy personality? Not in and of itself. I would say that real-self-being is a necessary but not a sufficient condition for healthy personality. Indeed, an authentic person may not be very "nice." In fact, he may seem much "nicer" socially and appear more mature and healthy when he is *not* being his real self than when he is his real self. But an individual's "obnoxious" but authentic self can never grow in the direction of greater maturity until the person has become acquainted with it and begins to *be* it. Real-self-being produces consequences which, in accordance with well known principles of behavior (cf. Skinner, 1953), produce changes in the real self. Thus, there can be no real growth of the self without real-self-being. Full disclosure of the self to at least one other significant human being appears to be one means by which a person discovers not only the breadth and depth of his needs and feelings, but also the nature of his own self-affirmed values. There is no necessary conflict, incidentally, between real-self-being and being an ethical or nice person, because for the average member of our society, self-owned ethics are generally acquired during the process of growing up. All too often, however, the self-owned ethics are buried under authoritarian morals (Fromm, 1947).

If self-disclosure is one of the means by which healthy personality is both achieved and maintained, we can also note that such activities as loving, psychotherapy, counseling, teaching, and nursing, all are impossible of achievement without the disclosure of the client. It is through self-disclosure that an individual reveals to himself and to the other party just exactly who, what, and where he is. Just as thermometers and sphygmomanometers disclose information about the real state of the body, self-disclosure reveals the real nature of the soul, or self. Such information is vital in order to conduct intelligent evaluations. All I mean by evaluation is comparing how a person is with some concept of optimum. You never really discover how truly sick your psychotherapy patient is until he discloses himself utterly to you. You cannot help your client in vocational guidance until he has disclosed to you something of the impasse in which he finds himself. You cannot love your spouse or your child or your friend unless those persons have permitted you to know them and to know what they need in order to move toward greater health and well-being. Nurses cannot nurse patients in any meaningful way unless they have permitted the patients to disclose their needs, wants, worries, anxieties and doubts, and so forth. Teachers cannot be very helpful to their students until they have permitted the students to disclose how utterly ignorant and misinformed they presently are. Teachers cannot even provide helpful information to the students until they have permitted the students to disclose exactly what they are interested in.

I believe we should reserve the term inter*personal* relationships to refer to transactions between "I and thou" (Buber, 1937), between *person* and *person*, not between role and role. A truly personal relationship between two people involves disclosure of self one to the other in full and spontaneous honesty. The data that we have collected up to the present time have shown us some rather interesting phenomena. We found (Jourard and Lasakow, 1958), for example, that the women we tested in universities in the Southeast were consistently higher self-disclosers than men; they seem to have a greater capacity for establishing person-to-person relationships, inter*personal* relationships, than men. This characteristic of women seems to be a socially-patterned phenomenon which sociologists (Parsons and Bales, 1955) refer to as the *expressive* role of women in contradistinction to the instrumental role which men universally are obliged to adopt. Men seem to be much more skilled at *impersonal, instrumental* role-playing. But public health officials, very concerned about the sex differential in mortality rates, have been wondering what it is about being a man which makes males die younger than females. Do you suppose that there is any connection whatsoever between the disclosure patterns of men and women and their differential death rates? I have already intimated that withholding self-disclosure seems to impose a certain stress on people. Maybe "being manly," whatever that means, is slow suicide! (See Chapter 6 on "Lethal Aspects of the Male Role.")

I think there is a very general way of stating the relationship between self-disclosure and assorted values such as healthy personality, physical health, group effectiveness, successful marriage, effective teaching, and effective nursing. It is this. A person's self is known to be the immediate determiner of his overt behavior. This is a paraphrase of the phenomenological point of view in psychology (Combs and Snygg, 1959). Now if we want to understand anything, explain it, control it, or predict it, it is helpful if we have available as much pertinent information as we possibly can. Self-disclosure provides a source of information which is relevant. This information has often been overlooked. Where it has not been overlooked, it has often been misinterpreted by observers and practitioners through such devices as projection or attribution. *It seems to be difficult for people to accept the fact that they do not know the very person whom they are confronting at any given moment.* We all seem to assume that we are expert psychologists and that we know the other person, when in fact we have only constructed a more or less autistic concept of him in our mind. If we are to learn more about man's self, then we must learn more about self-disclosure—its conditions, dimensions, and consequences. Beginning evidence (cf. Rogers, 1958) shows that actively accepting, empathic, loving, non-punitive response—in short, love—provides the optimum conditions under which man will disclose, or expose, his naked, quivering self to our gaze. It follows that if we would be helpful (or should I say *human*) we must grow to loving stature and learn, in Buber's terms, to confirm our fellow man in his very being. Probably, this presumes that we must *first* confirm our *own* being.

4

Sex and Openness in Marriage*

Let us talk first about something altogether rare—a happily married couple who love one another, not only in the sober sense of loving as Erich Fromm (1956) portrays it, but who can enjoy each other, delighting in one another's company. They know each other, care for and about one another, respond to the needs, actions, and emotions of the other, and respect each other's idiosyncrasies and uniqueness, not striving to sculpture each other into some image of what they are not. This is love according to Fromm, and for that matter, it is love even according to my own rather unromantic treatment of the theme (Jourard, 1958). I defined love, not as an emotion so much as freely expressed behavior, undertaken with the aim of fostering happiness and growth in the person loved. But there is something grim and joyless and even a sense of hard work implicit in that conception of love. I would like here to spice this conception with some laughter, some wholesome, lusty, fully expressed, mischievous, lecherous, saucy sex. Not sex as mere coupling, but sex as an expression of *joie-de-vivre*, of a sharing of the good things in life. Sex that is something deeply enjoyed, freely given and taken, with good, deep, soul-shaking climaxes, the kind that make a well-married couple look at each other from time to time, and either wink, or grin, or become humble at the remembrance of joys past and expectant of those yet to be enjoyed.

Marriage counselors and psychotherapists seldom hear about this kind of sex. For that matter, I suspect that it is rare for any of us to enjoy that sort of thing as a regular diet, though it would be a good thing if more of us did. While I cannot agree that sex solves anything, it surely

* Presented at the Workshop on Pastoral Counseling, University of Florida, February 1, 1961, and published in the *Journal of Humanistic Psychology*, October, 1961.

is a sensitive index or gauge of a person or of a relationship. Sex deteriorates with deterioration of the capacity of a person to establish a close, confiding, communicative, loving, non-sexual relationship with another person.

People marry for many reasons, and few people marry for love, because few people are able to love the person they marry at the time they marry them. In our society, people commonly marry in a romantic haze, usually ignorant of the traits, needs, and aims of their spouses. They marry an image, not a person. The image is partly a construction of their own needs and fantasies—much like the interpretations people make of a psychologist's ambiguous ink-blots—and partly a result of deliberate ambiguity or contrivance on the part of the other. The other person presents himself as the kind of person he thinks will be loved and accepted, but it is seldom really him. Following the ceremony, reality often sets in with an unpleasant shock. Certainly one of the reasons people marry—and there's really nothing wrong with this reason as such—is for sex. Our morality is such as to ensure that young people will be highly thwarted in a sexual sense at about the time they are supposed to marry. This is probably a good thing, because it provides a strong motive to bring people together.

Shortly after people are married, trouble begins, and it *should*, if the couple are growing people. Trouble is normal, to be expected, even desirable. It either begins in bed or else is reflected in bed. By and large, there are two broad classes of sexual difficulty, one growing out of prudery in its manifold forms and the other associated with impasses in the over-all relationship of a couple who, at one time, have been able to give and get sexual fulfillment with one another. I shall speak of each in turn. First, prudery.

SEXUAL DIFFICULTIES ARISING FROM PRUDERY

Dread or disgust are readily linked to sexuality in our culture. Young people are either kept in ignorance about the facts of life, or else they have the facts misrepresented to them. They may have heard some noisy, fully enjoyed sex play on the part of their parents, as part of

what Freud called the "primal scene," and misinterpreted
the mother's ecstatic groans or cries during the climax
as evidence of the father's brutality and the mother's
agony. Or, the mother may have silently, with martyred
air, implied to her daughter what pigs men are and what
a cross women have to carry. Or, the father may have
warned his son about venereal disease and about the
horrible ease of making girls pregnant. The daughter may
have been shielded from the baser facts of life—though
how this is possible today is hard to fathom. Let it suffice
for me to say that there is more opportunity for a young-
ster to grow up associating sexual love with guilt, sin,
pain, danger, filth, or disgust than to associate it with
responsible fun to be fully and freely enjoyed. Let such a
person marry. Though prudish, misinformed, or neuroti-
cally conditioned, such a person will have sex urges. But
sadly enough, a person who is unable gladly to acknowledge his own sexuality will find it very difficult to establish the open, communicative kind of relationship in
which love and sex flourish. Accordingly, the relationship
will likely reach an early impasse of sexual frustration for
both parties. Since neither one nor the other can get or
give full satisfaction in or out of bed, the relationship may
be dissolved or else become frozen into an impasse of
impersonal politeness or outright hostility and bitterness.
When people are sexually thwarted, it is hell. It is difficult to work, play, enjoy oneself or another person when
one is frustrated in this basic way. Moreover, sexual
frustration in marriage leads inevitably to anger and hostility, then to guilt for being angry—a vicious circle that
is difficult to break. Many a marriage that might have had
some chance to grow into a loving relationship has
foundered on the prudery arising from neurosis or ignorance in one spouse or the other. Some notion of the
misery that sexual privation can lead to may be seen in
the seldom discussed or even acknowledged misery of
husbands when their wives are pregnant. Some wives—
latent prudes—close the door on their husbands as soon
as the doctor confirms their pregnancy. They justify their
action on the seemingly righteous grounds that intercourse will jeopardize the baby. The fact is that except
for highly unusual cases, intercourse is feasible without

harm to the baby almost up into the eighth month if
not into the ninth. A good obstetrician can give authori-
tative advice in a matter like this. But many husbands
and wives are needlessly abstinent during the wife's
pregnancy, out of ignorance or prudery. Healthier couples
simply proceed until it gets awkward or medically unsafe.

Another outcome of prudery is stereotypy in lovemaking. Healthy spouses are experimental; they play at their
lovemaking. They explore the countless possible variations whenever they tire of some one position, and do so
without guilt or shame. It is not necessary to marital
happiness to do so, but if the inclination or whim hits
one spouse or the other to try something new, the more
healthy couples explore. And how a prude can spoil such
potentially delightful exploration! I have known couples
whose relationship deteriorated because one partner was
convinced the other was a pervert. The wife became repelled because her husband wanted to kiss her breasts, or
he was shocked to learn she entertained fantasies and
longings for a more active role in foreplay. Naturally, if
so-called forepleasures have become ends in themselves,
preferred over intercourse, then the individual is neurotic
or worse, but as aspects of sexual love in a good marriage,
diverse foreplay is to be encouraged if and as desired.
People who can acknowledge and accept their own sexuality in its breadth and depth can usually acknowledge
and accept the sexuality of their spouses in its potential
diversity.

Ignorance about contraception can ruin a potentially
healthy sex life, although again it takes an especial talent
today to be that ignorant. Continuous pregnancy probably is not too good for anybody concerned, though I
acknowledge that there are religious and ethical differences regarding the rightness of contraception. As an
individual I have no hesitation in affirming my own view
that contraception is a good thing, the while respecting
the contrary views of those who affirm other values. But
if a rich sex life is a value, and I assume it is, then I can
say that anxiety about unwanted pregnancy can ruin it.
Anxiety and sex are mutually exclusive. As a matter of
fact, there is probably an art to be learned in the use of
contraceptives, either on the part of the woman or the

man. Good sexual lovemaking is spontaneous or close to it. Stopping to "get ready" can dampen ardor and squelch a perfectly delightful impulse. The man or woman who employs a contraceptive device has to understand how it works, have confidence in its effectiveness, and yet somehow preserve the spontaneity and aesthetic values that are so easily destroyed by the necessity to become scientific and clinical. Prudery, reluctance to think clearly about this issue can either render contraceptives ineffective, or else make them effective, but destroy the fun or beauty of lovemaking.

Another aspect of lovemaking is aroma. Sex is an activity which brings people close to one another, to say the least. People smell! Given reasonable cleanliness, there will still be odors. Prudes who reject their own bodies generally are repelled by body odors, especially those musky smells that accompany sex. Healthier couples become even more excited by the odors of love which, in sober scientific language, arise in consequence of the responsiveness of the autonomic nervous system.

What can a minister do to help married people whose sexual difficulties are related to prudery? The first and most helpful thing he can do is seek to achieve a satisfactory sexual adjustment in his own marriage. Personal experience will not only enrich his marriage, but lend his presence the authority, unconscious attitudes, and relaxation that book-learning cannot provide. But becoming informed is valuable because information can frequently enlighten. I suspect, as a matter of fact, that members of a congregation who discuss sex with their minister and find him to be what Reich called sex-affirmative, that is, all for it, almost fall over with surprise. Certainly, anything which will reduce prudery in the pastoral counselor will be helpful. A reformed, rehabilitated prude can understand prudes better than could a more natural man, just as it takes an ex-alcoholic to help an alcoholic. Prudery, like love, is a many-splendored thing, taking many forms. I have by no means exhausted its protean potentials, but perhaps enough has been said on that source of destruction of married sexual love to give us some points for discussion, and now I will turn to impasses in the over-all marital relationship which naturally destroy mutual sex. I say "naturally" because it is obviously an artificial thing to try to discuss sex apart from a total relationship.

RELATIONSHIP IMPASSES AND SEXUAL DIFFICULTIES

A healthy relationship between two loving people is characterized by mutual knowledge, openness of communication, freedom to be oneself in the presence of the other without contrivance, and respect, to name but a few of the criteria (Jourard, 1958). When two people are thus open to one another, they will likewise have become able to be sexually open one with the other. But let an impasse arise, say, an unexpressed resentment, an unresolved argument, something unsaid, a feeling unexpressed, some departure from spontaneous openness, and it will inevitably make sexual lovemaking less probably fulfilling. Two newly married people who hardly know one another as persons may spend a lot of enjoyable time in bed with one another, but inevitably, the non-sexual aspects of marriage must be faced. As couples come gradually to know one another as persons rather than role-players (if they permit that much honest communication to occur), they may learn that they don't like each other or that they have apparently irreconcilable conflicts in values, goals, or needs. The sexual side of their marriage will certainly reflect this state of affairs. Very often, perhaps always, the earliest sign that a relationship outside the bedroom is reaching some unexpressed impasse is a cooling of ardor. The optimum in a marriage relationship, as in any relationship between persons is a relationship between I and Thou, where each partner is being himself in the transaction, without reserve, faking, or contrivance, disclosing himself as he is in a spirit of good will. This ideal is difficult and rarely achieved. In most relationships, it is experienced as moments of rare meeting, of communion. Certainly such moments, when *she* becomes truly *thou*, are experienced with joy. When one becomes Thou, a person, he or she becomes unpredictable, spontaneous, and the other becomes likewise spontaneous. At those times, or when two people are capable of such moments, their sex life will be exquisite.

This is almost to say that, given reasonable lack of prudery, a lusty, joyous, and yet holy and sometimes awe-inspiring sex life grows best out of a relationship between two persons who can be themselves with one another without fear of being deeply hurt when they are so unguarded. The same defenses which protect one from being hurt by one's spouse's remarks, deeds, or omissions are the very defenses which impede spontaneous sexuality. Openness before a person renders one open to sights, sounds, smells in the world, and also open to the riches of one's own feelings. The person who effectively guards himself against pain from the outside just as effectively ensures virtual sexual anesthesia.

One of the enemies of a healthy relationship between two spouses, and thus to any sexual fulfillment in the relationship, is a felt necessity to play formal roles in that relationship. While a division of labor is necessary to the effective functioning of any social system, including a family, it does not imply that husbands and wives must constantly be in a formal relationship with each other. When a person marries, is he marrying *that very person* of the opposite sex? Or a wife? If he is marrying a wife, then almost anybody who passes the test will do, because he is marrying a kit of tools and a counter of wares to be used, enjoyed, and consumed. He will pay for the services and enjoyments with money and with services, but this is very impersonal. It is only when two people can play their roles and yet be open, grow, change, that we can say they have a growing relationship. And it is such growing relationships that are compatible with good sex.

Many couples are terrified at growth, change in either themselves or in their spouses. This dread of growth manifests itself in many forms. One of the earliest signs that a person has outgrown a role in which he has been cast by the other person is a sense of boredom, of restlessness, of stultification, or boredom at the sameness of the other. He feels he would like to be different, but fears that if he expresses his difference, he will either lose love or hurt his spouse. A wife may have been passive, dependent, helpless early in the marriage, and was easily won by a dominant man whose identity as a man was reinforced by her helplessness. In time, she may discover that she has actually become more self-reliant, less eager to please, more able to assert difference. But if she is herself, expresses herself, she may render her spouse very insecure. If she has not consolidated her growth gains, her husband's reactions may frighten her back into the role in which *he* finds her most comfortable. Many marriages threaten to break up and many a sex life gets ruined because one of the spouses has grown more mature. "You aren't the sweet little thing I married," he may say, or, "When I married you, you seemed so strong and sure of yourself. Now, I find that you have weaknesses."

A pastoral counselor must, if he is to be helpful with such cases, have some notion, both from books and from his own personal experience, of what growthful changes, maturity in a person, look like. A person coming to himself, becoming himself, can raise hell for the spouse who is not growing as a person. And the hell of course spreads to bed. Uneven growth rates (I mean here growth as a person) have some different patterns. Among middle class people, the husband often remains hidden behind the mask of his manly role. The wife *may* grow discontented with her role before *he* gets dissatisfied with her role. As a matter of fact, it is my experience that problems brought to me as supposedly purely sex problems turn out inevitably to be problems that arise from fouled-up relationships. Growth and change in the persons who marry is inevitable and desirable. It never proceeds at the same rate or pace in the two partners. This means that impasses are inevitable and desirable because it is only in facing the impasses openly that each party keeps his knowledge of the other current and exposes himself to the opportunity to grow. Politeness and the hiding of discontent with one's role or with the behavior of the other are sure ways to destroy a relationship. As a matter of fact, once again we can look to the bedroom for the gauge of the relationship. A couple who are apparently compatible one with the other, but who harbor unexpressed resentment, will fail in the act.

I think that pastoral counselors will be most helpful in their task of midwifing marital well-being when and if they have themselves been able to face the breadth and depth of misery and joy in their own marriages, if they are growing persons rather than starched collars wearing the mask of a minister. There is surely nothing about being a minister which precludes being a person.

Yet, I cannot help making the observation that it must be very difficult indeed to be oneself, to be a person, while one is a minister, so great is the pressure from others and from the self to play a role. In ministers or their wives with whom I have conferred as therapist, I have been amazed and saddened at the stresses and strains under which they are obliged to live and work. Because the ministry plays such an important role in the well-being of people in a community, I think ministers do themselves and the public a disservice when they cannot find occasions and people where they can simply be themselves, "offstage," as it were. I believe that the ministry should have, as part of its organization, a full-time psychotherapist readily available to help individual ministers and their families grow as persons. This would certainly help render them not only more effective in their professional functions, but also much happier in their personal and marital lives.

5

Experience, Self-Disclosure, and the Writer*

There is a distinction between an authentic writer and a propagandist. A propagandist seeks to transmit deliberately falsified accounts of reality to people, so that they will form beliefs and attitudes that are useful to the propagandist or to the man who pays this craftsman. The propagandist seeks to diminish people. He has a vested interest in their remaining stupid, misinformed, or uncritical. An authentic writer, whether he be poet, reporter, novelist, essayist, playwright, or short-story writer, seeks instead to reveal his personal experience of some aspect of the world in ways that will be understood and reacted to by mature, whole people. He discloses his experiencing in effective or artful ways, with no aim other than being faithful to this experiencing. Tacitly or openly, he addresses himself to people who can be enlarged; he wants to enrich their experience. He writes for the "clerisy." If he makes money at it, or achieves fame, that is because of the accident that, at that time and in that place, people treasure truth when it is artfully presented.

Now I would like to draw a distinction between experience and self-disclosure. Experience here refers to a process—to the flow of feelings, perceptions, memories, and fantasies as these occur from moment to moment. The only person who can ever know a man's experience directly is the individual himself. Whether he reveals this to another person depends upon many factors, as we are beginning to discover. For example, the subject matter to be disclosed, the relation of the audience to the discloser, characteristics of the audience, and individual characteristics of the potential discloser are all factors known to

* This paper was presented as a talk to the Gainesville Writer's League, Gainesville, Florida, September 18, 1962.

40

influence whether or not an individual will reveal his experiential flow to another.

Everybody has his unique experience of the world, but some experience it with more intensity of feeling, in new dimensions, and with greater grasp of meaning than others. Hopefully, those who write will fall into the semi-aristocratic camp of the intense experiencers. Literature would be in a sorry state if only those wrote who experienced the world in banal, crude, and unimaginative ways.

But writing—authentic writing as opposed to propaganda—like all forms of authentic disclosure of experience, entails risk. The chief risk in writing is letting other people know how one has experienced the events impinging on one's life. All that other people can ever see of an individual is that highly expurgated version of himself that is made public through actions and clichéd pronouncements. As we know only too well, a man's public utterances are frequently different, radically different, from what he authentically feels and believes. Many of us dread being known because we fear that if we were thus known by others—as intimately as we know our own experience—we would be divorced, fired, imprisoned, shot, or otherwise harmed.

A writer may behave in public just like a Babbitt, or a suburban nonentity, and yet record his authentic experiencing in print. In so doing, he runs risks from the reactions of his neighbors, his friends, his family, and others. This is so because if he is true to his calling, that of authentic recorder and reporter of his own experience, he will inevitably show aspects of himself and his personal reactions to others and events that are not ordinarily revealed in everyday behavior. I am sure that the people in the little town in North Carolina with whom Thomas Wolfe grew up were not aware of the intensity and meaning of his experience of them, and the many lawsuits Wolfe was involved in showed some of the risks of disclosure.

A writer, if he is to be effective, should have a large and sensitive soul. Stated another way, he should be capable of "registering" more facets of the effects of existence upon him than the average person. He must also, of course, have the courage to be, that is, to disclose

his experience in spite of censure, risk, economic privation, and the like. I do not like much of what Henry
Miller says about Jews, for example, but I believe that
he is reporting his experience faithfully and is thereby
enriching my experience, helping me to sharpen my sense
of my own identity—permitting me to agree, disagree,
compare, and contrast my experiencing with his.

This is a curious thing about experiencing which we
psychologists are just starting to learn. (We are slow in
this respect, lagging behind artists, but we are methodical
and steady.) We are learning that sharing one's authentic
experiencing with another person has important effects
upon both the discloser and the listener. Many a patient
undergoing psychotherapy comes to understand his existence and to assume responsibility for its future course as
a consequence of revealing himself fully to another
human being—his therapist. I have little doubt but that
we therapists have lost the chance to make some professional fees because a prospective patient came to achieve
catharsis, insight into and compassion for himself, through
writing a poem, a novel, a play. Disclosure of one's being
can be therapeutic.

But by the same token, the person who reads or listens
to the hitherto concealed authentic experience of another
is enriched by it. To learn of another's experiencing is to
broaden and deepen the dimensions of one's own experience. In ways that we do not yet fully understand, at
least in a scientific sense, the disclosed experience of the
other person enables us to see things, feel things, imagine
things, hope for things that we could never even have
imagined before we were exposed to the revelations of
the discloser. Since we are all similar to one another in
basic respects, as well as unique in others, we can understand another's off-beat experiencing if it is fully and
effectively disclosed; the vicarious experience that reading
or listening provides us with can shape our essence,
change us, just as first-hand experience can. Experience
seems to be as transfusable as blood, and it can be as
invigorating. Hence, the slogan *Humani nihil a me
alienum puto*. Politicians know that shared experience
can affect people, and so dictators make pains to extermi-
nate or gag sensitive experiencers who are vocal. They

may do this literally, or else render them ineffective by giving them a vested interest in the wealth of the state. More than one good poet, playwright, or novelist has had his experiencing edge blunted by wealth or success; or he has sold his soul for a position on the Book of the Month roster.

Man's capacity to experience the world in subtle and fully described ways is probably the fount of new discovery, both of nature and of man. There was a motto written on the paper back books we bought for philosophy courses when I was an undergraduate—cheap copies of Berkeley, Hume, Locke, and others. The motto read, "To be able to say what other men only think and feel is what makes poets and sages." Now Nabokov, with his account of Humbert in pursuit of Lolita, accentuated in me a dim feeling that would always have been latent and unverbalized and unacknowledged. I never really appreciated the beauty of a nymphet before he called it to my attention. Probably somewhere a young man sits, enthralled with the erotic potentials of 85-year-old women, looking for the courage and the art to disclose his experience so that his fellow men can be awakened to a hitherto dim feeling.

One of the magnificent things about Pasternak, to my way of thinking, was his ability to maintain a personal experience of life in a political prison; he saw himself as a person, not a tool of the state. He had the courage to disclose this experience in spite of great risks. Frankl, too, clung to human personal modes of experiencing in a death camp, and resisted the dehumanizing forces present. We might say that authentic writers help to protect something very precious in a people, namely, their capacity to continue experiencing life in personal ways, as persons rather than as functionaries of the state, a business, or a corporation. A writer provides his reader with a role-model, both of the courage to experience without dimming or repressing this or that facet of self, and the courage to share this experiencing with others.

Now, let me make some observations about the act of writing. The act of writing of one's experience bears something in common with the act of love. The writer, at his most productive moments, just flows. He gives of that which is uniquely himself. He makes himself naked, recording his nakedness in the written word. Herein lies, to my way of thinking, some of the terror which frequently freezes a writer, preventing him from producing. Herein, too, lies some of the courage that must be entailed in letting others learn how one has experienced or is experiencing the world. Dried-up writers have confessed to me that they are often impotent in bed, and I suspect that both types of impotence stem from similar reasons. In each case, it stems from a dread to reveal some aspect of the self to one other person, or to a whole reading public. There is a lack of courage to acknowledge some flaw or foible to self and others. The consequence seems to be that in seeking to block off the flaw, a person blocks off, as well, his creative or his loving flow.

There is another parallel between authentic writing and loving that has come to my attention. The openness or receptivity to experience that seems so essential to the "material-gathering" stage of any writing assignment is not so different a mode of experiencing from the openness of a lover to his loved one. A loving man (or woman) opens all his senses, drops his defenses, in order to be maximally affected by his loved one. This is why a mature lover can tell you more about his loved one than anyone else can. He is more open to her. He can also be hurt by her more than by anyone else, incidentally. But this is only the intake side of the intake-output equation of writing and loving. The lover responds to his loved one with a spontaneous expression of his authentic being. He does not hold back, but is instead transparent during his transactions with his loved one. By the same token, the writer, at the moment of writing, is making his experience available to his potential audience. If he tries to hold back, it seems he plugs up the verbal flow that must get set down on paper. The difference between the dialogue of love and the attenuated dialogue of writing is that the writer has an opportunity to correct and amend his statement before it gets seen by the world. Incidentally, this correction may be one of the basic differences between art and verbal diarrhea or irresponsible self-expressiveness.

I have often wondered about a writer's concept of his

reader, as he sits at his table writing of his experience. Does he see his reader as a nitwit? As an enemy? I think Freud saw his readers as somewhat hostile—perhaps rightly so. I think women's magazine fiction-writers and television writers have a contemptuous view of their readers' or viewers' capacities to profit from authentic experience. Certainly, the characters are only paper-thin, with conflicts that fall short of true, human tragedy.

Probably it is true that if a writer expresses himself in the way that, to him, seems most faithfully to convey his unique experience his audience will stretch or bend to encounter him. Again, this takes courage, because people, in writing or talking, somehow get the idea that *only* if they carve the unique edges off their experience and fit it into preconceived molds will they be understood. This attitude denies the capacity of the audience to stretch. Creative people grope for the new forms that will carry their experience; witness the literary experiments of Virginia Woolf, James Joyce, or Kenneth Patchen. Less creative people jam experience into Procrustean molds.

A good question I like to ask of any person, whether he is a writer or of some other calling, is this: Am I diminished, unaffected, or enlarged after my encounter with him? Here are some writers who have enhanced my being and increased my sense of myself and my grasp of the world—Faulkner, Pasternak, Frankl, Kazantzakis, Steinbeck, Hemingway, Camus, Freud, Buber, Carl Rogers, Abe Maslow, Sartre, Arthur Miller, Tennessee Williams, Frank Taylor, Hugh McClennan, Dylan Thomas, and T. S. Eliot. All of these writers addressed me, and reached me, and changed me. I think all of them have been unique experiencers of life, and honest and artful portrayers of this experience. They are authentic writers.

6

Some Lethal Aspects
of the Male Role*

Men die sooner than women, and so health scientists
and public health officials have become justly concerned
about the sex difference in death age. Biology provides
no convincing evidence to prove that female organisms
are instrinsically more durable than males, or that tissues
or cells taken from males are less viable than those taken
from females. A promising place to look for an explanation of the perplexing sex-differential in mortality is in
the transactions between men and their environments,
especially their interpersonal environments. In principle,
there must be ways of behaving among people which
prolong a man's life and insure his fuller functioning, and
ways of behaving which speed a man's progress toward
death. The present paper is devoted to an overview of
some aspects of being a man in American society which
may be related to man's acknowledged faster rate of dying.

The male role, as personally and socially defined, re-
quires man to appear tough, objective, striving, achieving,
unsentimental, and emotionally unexpressive. But seeming is not being. If a man *is* tender (behind his *persona*),
if he weeps, if he shows weakness, he will likely be viewed
as unmanly by others, and he will probably regard himself as inferior to other men.

Now, from all that we can fathom about the *subjective*
side of man, as this has been revealed in autobiography,
novels, plays, and psychotherapists' case histories, it seems
true that men are as capable as women at responding to
the play of life's events with a broad range of feelings.
Man's potential thoughts, feelings, wishes and fantasies

* Adapted from a paper presented at a symposium entitled
"The Compleat Man," held at the Southeastern Psychological
Association, Atlanta, Georgia, April, 1960.

know no bounds, save those set by his biological structure and his personal history. But the male role, and the male's self-structure will not allow man to acknowledge or to express the entire breadth and depth of his inner experience, to himself or to others. Man seems obliged, rather, to hide much of his real self—the ongoing flow of his spontaneous inner experience—from himself and from others.

MANLINESS AND LOW SELF-DISCLOSURE

Research in patterns of self-disclosure has shown that men typically reveal less personal information about themselves to others than women (Jourard 1961a; Jourard and Lasakow, 1958; Jourard and Landsman, 1960; Jourard and Richman, 1963). Since men, doubtless, have as much "self," i.e., inner experience, as women, then it follows that men have more "secrets" from the interpersonal world than women. It follows further that men, seeming to dread being known by others, must be more continually tense (neuromuscular tension) than women. It is as if "being manly" implies the necessity to wear neuromuscular "armor," the character armor which Reich (1948) wrote about with such lucidity. Moreover, if a man has "secrets," "something to hide," it must follow that other people will be a threat to him; they might pry into his secrets, or he may, in an unguarded moment, reveal his true self in its nakedness, thereby exposing his areas of weakness and vulnerability. Naturally, when a person is in hostile territory, he must be continually alert, hypertonic, opaque, and restless. All this implies that trying to seem manly is a kind of "work," and work imposes stress and consumes energy. Manliness, then, seems to carry with it a chronic burden of stress and energy-expenditure which could be a factor related to man's relatively shorter life-span.

If self-disclosure is an empirical index of "openness," of "real-self being," and if openness and real-self being are factors in health and wellness, then the research in self-disclosure seems to point to one of the potentially lethal aspects of the male role. Men keep their selves to themselves, and impose thereby an added burden of stress

beyond that imposed by the exigencies of everyday life.
The experience of psychosomatic physicians who under-
take psychotherapy with male patients suffering peptic
ulcers, essential hypertension and kindred disorders seems
to support this contention. Psychotherapy is the art of
promoting self-disclosure and authentic being in patients
who withhold their real selves from expression, and
clinical experience shows that when psychotherapy has
been effective with psychosomatic patients, the latter
change their role-definitions, their self-structures, and
their behavior in the direction of greater spontaneity and
openness, with salutory consequences to their bodies.
The time is not far off when it will be possible to demonstrate with adequately controlled experiments the nature
and degree of correlation between levels and amounts of
self-disclosure, and proneness to illness and/or an early
death age.

MANLINESS: THE LACK OF INSIGHT AND EMPATHY

There is another implication of the fact that men are
lower self-disclosers than women, an implication that relates to self-insight. Men, trained by their upbringing to
assume the "instrumental role," tend more to relate to
other people on an *I—It* basis than women (Buber,
1937).[1] They are more adept than women at relating

[1] There is an interesting implication of these observations for
the training of male psychotherapists. It seems true that effective psychotherapists of whatever theoretical school are adept
at establishing a warm, bilaterally communicative relationship
with their patients, one characterized by a refraining from
manipulation on the part of the therapist. The effective therapists do not "take over" the patient's problems, or "solve
them" for the patient. Rather, they seem to "be and to let
be" (Rogers, 1958). This mode of being is quite alien to the
modal male. Indeed, it can be discerned among beginning
therapists that there is often considerable dread of such passivity, because it constitutes a threat to masculine identity.
Beginning therapists seem to be most fascinated by "manly,"
active techniques such as hypnosis, reflection, interpretation,
etc.—the kinds of things which will be difficult for them to
master, but which will make them feel they are *doing something*
to the patient which will get him well. These techniques, however, leave the self of the therapist hidden behind the mask of
his professional role, and have limited effectiveness.

impersonally to others, seeing them as the embodiment of their roles rather than as persons enacting roles. Women (often to the despair of business-like men) seem to find it difficult to keep their interpersonal relationships *im*personal; they sense and respond to the feelings of the *other* person even in a supposedly official transaction, and they respond to their *own* feelings toward the other person, seeming to forget the original purpose of the impersonal transaction.

Now, one outcome that is known to follow from effective psychotherapy (which, it will be recalled, entails much self-disclosure from the patient to the therapist) is that the patient becomes increasingly sensitized to the nuances of his own feelings (and those of the therapist) as they ebb and flow in the relationship. The patient becomes more adept at labeling his feelings (Dollard and Miller, 1950, pp. 281-304), diagnosing his own needs, and understanding his own reactions. Co-incident with this increase in insight is an increase in empathy into others, an increase in his ability to "imagine the real" (Buber, 1957). Studies of leadership show that the leaders of the most effective groups maintain an optimum "distance" from their followers, avoiding the distraction thereby of overly intimate personal knowledge of the followers' immediate feelings and needs (Fiedler, 1957). But not all of a man's everyday life entails the instrumental leadership role. For example, a man may "lead" his family, but he is not a father twenty-four hours a day. Personal life calls both for insight and for empathy. If practice at spontaneous self-disclosure promotes insight and empathy, then perhaps we have here one of the mechanisms by which women become more adept at these aspects of their so-called "expressive" role. Women, trained toward motherhood and a comforting function both engage in and receive more self-disclosure than men (Jourard and Richman, 1963).

Let us now focus upon insight, in the sense that we have used the term here. If men are trained, as it were, to ignore their own feelings, in order more adequately to pursue the instrumental aspects of manliness, it follows that they will be less sensitive to what one might call "all is not well signals," as these arise in themselves. It is probably a fact that in every case of outright physical or mental illness, earlier signs occurred which, if noted and acted upon, would have averted the eventual breakdown. Vague discomfort, boredom, anxiety, depression probably arose as consequences of the afflicted person's way of life, but because these signals were "weak," or else deliberately or automatically ignored, the illness-conducive way of life persisted until breakdown finally forced a respite, a withdrawal from the illness-producing role. The hypothesis may be proposed that women, more sensitized to their inner experience, will notice their "all is not well signals" sooner and more often than men, and change their mode of existence to one more conducive to wellness, e.g., consult a doctor sooner, or seek bed-rest more often than men. Men, by contrast, fail to notice these "all is not well signals" of weaker intensity, and do not stop work, nor take to their beds until the destructive consequences of their manly way of life have progressed to the point of a "stroke," or a total collapse. It is as if women "amplify" such inner distress signals even when they are dim, while men, as it were, "tune them out" until they become so strong, they can no longer be ignored.

Accordingly, manly men, unaccustomed to self-disclosure, and characterized by lesser insight and lesser empathy than women, do violence to their own unique needs, and persist in modes of behavior which to be sure, are effective at changing the world, but no less effective in modifying their "essence" from the healthy to the moribund range.

A curious exception to these patterns has been noted among college males. Mechanic and Volkart (1961, p. 52) have proposed the term "illness behavior" to describe "the way in which symptoms are perceived, evaluated, and acted upon by a person who recognizes some pain, discomfort, or other sign of organic malfunction." Visiting a physician at a university infirmary following perception of some malaise thus qualifies as a type of "illness behavior." Some as yet unpublished research at the University of Florida Student Infirmary (20) has shown that male students consulted the infirmary one and one half times more frequently than comparable female students during the year under study. A breakdown according to religious denomination showed, moreover, that of the "high users" of the Infirmary, Jewish male students were represented with nearly double the frequency of males affiliated with Methodist, Baptist, Catholic, and other religious groups. A completely independent study (Jourard, 1961b) of self-disclosure patterns among members of different religious denominations on the University of Florida campus showed that Jewish males were significantly higher disclosers than were comparable Methodist, Baptist, and Catholic males, none of the latter three groups differing significantly from one another. These findings imply that college males in general, and Jewish college males in particular, may depart from more stereotyped patterns of masculinity which prevail in the general population for the age range between 18 and 23.

MANLINESS AND INCOMPETENCE AT LOVING

Loving, including self-love, entails knowledge of the unique needs and characteristics of the loved person (Fromm, 1956). To know another person calls for empathy *in situ*, the capacity to "imagine the real," and the ability to "let be," that is, to permit and promote the disclosure of being. The receipt of disclosure from another person obviously must enhance one's factual knowledge about him, and also it must improve one's degree of empathy into him. But data obtained in the systematic study of self-disclosure has shown, not only that men disclose less to others than women, but also that of all the disclosure that does go on among people, *women are the recipients of more disclosure than men* (Jourard and Richman, 1963). This fact helps one better to understand why men's concepts of the subjective side of other people—of other men as well as of women and children —are often naïve, crude, or downright inaccurate. Men are often alleged, in fiction, to be mystified by the motives for the behavior of others, motives which a woman observer can understand instantly, and apparently intuitively. If this conjecture is true, it should follow that men, in spite of good intentions to promote the happiness and growth of others by loving actions, will often "miss the

target." That is, they will want to make the other person
happy, but their guesses about the actions requisite to
the promotion of this goal will be inappropriate, and their
actions will appear awkward or crude.

The obverse of this situation is likewise true. If a man
is reluctant to make himself known to another person,
even to his spouse—because it is not manly thus to be
psychologically naked—then it follows that *men will be
difficult to love.* That is, it will be difficult for a woman
or another man to know the immediate present state of
the man's self, and his needs will thereby go unmet.
Some men are so skilled at dissembling, at "seeming,"
that even their wives will not know when they are lonely,
bored, anxious, in pain, thwarted, hungering for affection, etc. And the men, blocked by pride, dare not disclose their despair or need.

The situation extends to the realm of self-love. If true
love of self implies behavior which will truly meet one's
own needs and promote one's own growth, then men
who lack profound insight, or clear contact with their
real selves will be failures at self-loving. Since they do
not know what they feel, want and need (through long
practice at repression) men's "essences" will show the
results of self-neglect, or harsh treatment of the self by
the self.

It is a fact that suicide, mental illness, and death occur
sooner and more often among "men whom nobody
knows" (that is, among unmarried men, among "lone
wolves") than among men who are loved as individual,
known persons, by other individual, known persons. Perhaps loving and being loved enables a man to take his
life seriously; it makes his life take on value, not only to
himself, but also to his loved ones, thereby adding to its
value for him. Moreover, if a man is open to his loved
one, it permits two people—he and his loved one—to
examine, react to, diagnose, evaluate, and do something
constructive about *his* inner experience and his present
condition when these fall into the undesirable range.
When a man's self is hidden from everybody else, even
from a physician, it seems also to become much hidden
even from himself, and it permits entropy—disease and
death—to gnaw into his substance without his clear

knowledge. Men who are unknown and/or inadequately loved often fall ill, or even die as if suddenly and without warning, and it is a shock and a surprise to everyone who hears about it. One wonders why people express surprise when they themselves fall ill, or when someone else falls ill or dies, apparently suddenly. If one had direct access to the person's real self, one would have had many earlier signals that the present way of life was generating illness. Perhaps, then, the above-noted "inaccessibility" (Rickers-Ovsiankina, 1956) of man, in addition to hampering his insight and empathy, also handicaps him at self-loving, at loving others and at being loved. If love is a factor that promotes life, then handicap at love, a male characteristic, seems to be another lethal aspect of the male role.

THE MALE ROLE AND DISPIRITATION

Frankl (1955) has argued that unless a man can see meaning and value in his continuing existence, his morale will deteriorate, his immunity will decrease, and he will sicken more readily, or even commit suicide. Schmale (1958) noted that the majority of a sample of patients admitted to a general hospital suffered some depressing disruption in object relations prior to the onset of their symptoms. Extrapolating from many observations and opinions of this sort, the present writer proposed a theory of inspiration-dispiration. Broadly paraphrased, this theory holds that, when a man finds hope, meaning, purpose, and value in his existence, he may be said to be "inspirited," and isomorphic brain events weld the organism into its optimal, anti-entropic mode of organization. "Dispiriting" events, perceptions, beliefs, or modes of life tend to weaken this optimum mode of organization (which at once sustains wellness, and mediates the fullest, most effective functioning and behavior), and illness is most likely to flourish then. It is as if the body, when a man is dispirited, suddenly becomes an immensely fertile "garden" in which viruses and germs proliferate like jungle vegetation. In inspirited states, viruses and germs find a man's body a very uncongenial milieu for unbridled growth and multiplication.

Now, from what has been said in previous sections, it seems clear that the male role provides many opportunities for dispiritation to arise. The best example is provided by the data on aging. It is a well-documented observation that men in our society, following retirement, will frequently disintegrate and die not long after they assume their new life of leisure. It would appear that masculine identity and self-esteem—factors in inspiritation for men —are predicated on a narrow base. If men can see themselves as manly, and life as worth-while, only so long as they are engaged in gainful employ, or are sexually potent, or have enviable social status, then clearly these are tenuous bases upon which to ground one's existence. It would seem that women can continue to find meaning, and *raisons d'être* long after men feel useless and unneeded.

Thus, if man's sense of masculine identity, as presently culturally defined, is a condition for continued existence, and if this is easily undermined by the vicissitudes of aging or the vicissitudes of a changing social system, then, indeed, the male role has an added lethal component. The present writer has known men who became dispirited following some financial or career upset, and who fell victims to some infectious disease, or "heart failure" shortly thereafter. Their wives, though affected by the husbands' reverses or death, managed to find new grounds and meaning for continued existence, and got on with living.

DISCUSSION AND SUMMARY

It has been pointed out that men, lower disclosers of self than women, are less insightful and empathic, less competent at loving, and more subject to dispiritation than women. The implication of these aspects of manliness for health and longevity was explored. As a concluding note, it seems warranted to step back, and look briefly at the problem of roles from a broader perspective.

Social systems need to delimit people's behavior in order to keep the systems functioning. No social system can use all of every man's self, and yet keep the social system functioning well. This is what roles are for—sex roles as well as occupational, age, and familial roles. The role-definitions help men and women to learn just which actions they must perform, and which they must suppress in order to keep the social system functioning properly. But it should not then be thought that just because society cannot use all that a man is, that the man should then strive to root out all self that is neither useful, moral, or in vogue.

If health, full-functioning, happiness and creativity are valued goals for mankind, then laymen and behavioral scientists alike must seek ways of redefining the male role, to help it become less restrictive and repressive, more expressive of the "compleat" man, and more conducive to life.

Part III

Role of Authenticity in Helping Others

7

I-Thou Relationship versus Manipulation in Counseling and Psychotherapy*

There is ample evidence today that man *can* mold and structure the behavior of his fellow man according to some predetermined scheme. We need point only to such phenomena as "teaching machines," Chinese "thought reform," Dale Carnegie's ways of "winning" friends, "hidden persuaders," political propaganda, "subliminal advertisements" on television, and, of course, the centuries-old techniques employed by women to make men see, feel, believe, and do what they want them to. The question germane to this symposium is, "Can techniques for the manipulation of behavior, of demonstrated effectiveness in the rat-laboratory, the market-place, and the boudoir, be deliberately employed in the arts of counseling and psychotherapy?" It will be my contention in the remainder of my presentation that "behavioristic" approaches to counseling and psychotherapy rightly acknowledge man's susceptibility to manipulation by another man, but they ignore the possibly deleterious impact of such manipulation on the whole man. Moreover, the would-be manipulator of a man, whether counselor, therapist, advertiser, politician, propagandist, or woman may be doing violence, not only to his target, *but also to himself*.

Today, we are almost at the point of being able to program therapy in the same manner that academic learning can be programmed with so-called teaching-machines (Skinner, 1958). We are beginning to get some notions

* Adapted from a paper presented at a symposium on "Behavioristic Approaches to Counseling and Psychotherapy," Southeastern Psychological Association, St. Augustine, Florida, April 25, 1959, and published in the *Journal of Individual Psychology*, Vol. 15, 1959, pp. 174-179.

of what healthy personality looks like (Jourard, 1958) and what health-yielding behavior might be. It is tempting, therefore, to imagine some such situation as a therapist flashing a light, or a smile, or a glance at the patient whenever the latter emits behavior thought to be health-promoting. If these stimuli have become reinforcing, he thus will increase the rate of wellness-yielding behavior in his presence and weaken those responses which produced and perpetuated symptoms. In fact, if such a procedure were desirable, one might construct an automatic therapy-machine, somewhat as follows: whenever the patient talks about subject matter which leaves him "cold" and unemotional, a light remains off. The patient's job is to get the light on and keep it on. As soon as he discusses emotionally meaningful material, his autonomic responses will close switches that turn on the light. Shades of 1984! Then, the therapist can go fishing, and the patient will subsequently display healthy behavior whenever he encounters a machine. Monstrous though these ideas sound to me, yet they are not implausible. Greenspoon (1955) and numerous workers following his lead (cf. Krasner, 1958) have demonstrated the power of a well-placed verbal reinforcer to increase the rate at which selected verbal operants are emitted. What is wrong with aiming toward the eventual control of patients' behavior *in situ* by means of reinforcements deliberately administered by the therapist?

I am afraid that a program of psychotherapy undertaken with such an aim is a contradiction in terms. It cannot achieve the aim of fostering a patient's growth toward healthier personality, one aspect of which, I believe, is healthy interpersonal behavior. It cannot achieve such therapeutic aims purely *because* it constitutes deliberate manipulation of man by man. Such is not a healthy interpersonal transaction, according to criteria I have outlined elsewhere (Jourard, 1958). I believe, and I am not alone in this belief, that man is sick—not just neurotic and psychotic people, but so-called "normal" man too—because he hides his real self in his transactions with others. He relates impersonally to others and to himself. He equates his roles in the social system with his identity and tries to deny the existence of all real self which is irrelevant to role or self-concept. In my opinion, the aim of psychotherapy is not so much that of remitting salient symptoms as it is to alter interpersonal behavior from that range which generates the symptoms (manipulating self and others), to a pattern which generates and maintains healthy personality. A convenient name for such growth-yielding behavior is real-self behavior, or real-self interpersonal behavior, and it is contrasted with faking, seeming, play-acting, or contrived interpersonal behavior—that is, straining after effect, or manipulating oneself in order to appear to be what one is *not*.

If we look naïvely at the psychotherapeutic situation, we observe a patient talking about himself to his therapist. At first, the patient is trying to manipulate the therapist's perceptions of him. But the latter listens and seems to avoid conventional responses to what is told him, such as scolding, shock, scorn, and moral indignation. Encouraged by the lack of expected censure, the patient may go on spontaneously to reveal all manner of things about himself. One gathers he had never before in his life told these things or expressed these feelings to anyone. In fact, in the therapy situation, that patient remembers things which surprise him; he experiences feelings that never before had he even envisioned. As time goes on, he becomes remarkably free in expressing what is passing through his mind, and if late in therapy you asked him to describe himself, he would give a much more comprehensive picture of his wishes, feelings, and motives than he might have earlier in the game. Outside the therapy room, people who have known him notice that he has changed in that he seems less tense, more able to acknowledge a broader range of motives, and often much more spontaneous in his behavior with others. Moreover, he seems to be much more "genuine" in his dealings with others. The absence of his symptoms becomes almost incidental in the face of the more basic changes that seem to have gone on.

What has been responsible for these changes which sometimes take place?

The man has gone through a unique experience which

evidently *has* changed his behavior from responses that generated and perpetuated "symptoms" to responses which yield more valued outcomes.

This seems to be the experience of being permitted to *be*—to be himself; the experience of being utterly attended to by a professional man who is of good will, who seeks to understand him utterly and to communicate both his good will and his understanding *as these grow*. It is the experience of feeling free to be and to disclose himself in the presence of another human person whose good will is assured, but whose responses are unpredictable. Recent studies, summarized by Carl Rogers (1958), have shown that it is not the technique or the theoretical orientation of the therapist which fosters growth of the sort I have been describing. Rather it is the manner of the therapist's *being* when in the presence of the patient. *Effective* therapists seem to follow this implicit hypothesis: If they *are themselves* in the presence of the patient, avoiding *compulsions* to silence, to reflection, to interpretation, to impersonal technique, and kindred character disorders, but instead striving to know their patient, involving themselves in his situation, and then responding to his utterances with their spontaneous selves, this fosters growth. In short, they love their patients. They employ their powers in the service of their patient's well-being and growth, not inflict them on him. Somehow there is a difference.

But this loving relationship is a far cry from the impersonal administration of reflections, interpretations, or the equivalent of pellets. The loving therapist is quite free and spontaneous in his relationship: his responses are bound only by his ethics and his judgment. He may laugh, scold, become angry, give advice—in short, break most of the rules laid down in psychotherapy training manuals. This differs sharply from the deliberate restriction of therapist-behavior to some range thought to be health-fostering. Such restriction of behavior by therapists makes them the legitimate butt of jokes and caricatures (Haley, 1958); they become so *predictable*. Evidently it is only the therapist's good will which needs to be predictable, not his specific responses to a patient's disclosures.

It is my growing opinion, somewhat buttressed by

accumulating experience in my own therapeutic work, that valued change—growth—in patients is fostered when the therapist is a rather free individual functioning as a person with all of his feelings and fantasies as well as his wits. I am coming to believe that the therapist who strives to remain a thinking, and *only* thinking, creature in the therapeutic situation is a failure at promoting growth. Incidentally, in our concern with what we do to clients and patients we have never asked what we do to ourselves. What is the impact of therapy on the *therapist?* The "technical" therapist is striving to manipulate himself and his patient rather than *respond* to him. He is thus perpetuating his own detachment from most of his real self. He does this by striving to be a good disciple of his master or practitioner of his technique. My patients have been vociferous in deploring those times when I have experimented with manipulation. I have tried delimiting my behavior to the dispensing of reflections of feelings. I did a pretty good job of it, too. I have tried imposing the fundamental rule on patients, remaining silent except for well-timed utterance of *ex cathedra* interpretations. I have, I confess, even tried deliberately to shape my patient's behavior in the therapy hour with some rather ingeniously discovered reinforcers which varied from patient to patient, e.g., the "head-bob" when the output was "right," looking away from the patient's face whenever he was uttering what I thought would be most helpful, and so on. The only trouble with these gimmicks was that in time the patients would "see through them" and become quite angered at being manipulated in those ways. I am beginning to think that people, even patients, resent being manipulated. I know I do. I become furious when, for example, a salesman gives me a canned pitch which his supervisor told him "worked" in some percentage of cases. I can't stand a Dale Carnegie smile or any of the other departures from simple, spontaneous honesty and revelation of real self in a relationship between man and man. There is something downright degrading in being treated like a boob or a ninny, as something less than fully human. I have come to recognize, too, that those who habitually withhold their real selves from others, and instead strive to manipulate them in one way or another, do violence to their own integrity as well as to that of their victim. Surely, behavior that doesn't do a bit of good for the therapist can't do much good for his patient. We need data on this point.

Buber (1937) has succinctly summed up these observations with his concepts of the *I-Thou* relationship and the *dialogue*. Surely, our patients come to us because they have become so estranged from their real selves that they are incapable of making these known to their associates in life. I don't see how we can re-acquaint our patients with their real selves by striving to subject them to subtle manipulations and thus to withhold *our* real selves from them. It reminds me of the sick leading the sick. In point of fact, if my experience means anything, it has shown me that *the closest I can come to eliciting and reinforcing real-self behavior in my patient is by manifesting it myself.* This presumes that I am able to do this. Probably, in virtue of my own training, and whatever was real in my own therapy, I am better able to do this than an untrained person.

However, my permitting myself to "be real," to be a real person in response to my patient while I am yet committed to his wellness, is a far cry from deliberately sitting down with myself, or a colleague, to plot my strategy for eliciting behavior from him which might make him well. When a therapist is *committed* to the task of helping a patient grow, he functions as a whole person, and not as a disembodied intellect, computer, or reinforcement programmer. He strives to know his patient by hearing him out. He does not limit his behavior to some range prescribed by theory or cook book. He does, however, retain his separate identity, and he is thus able to see and understand things which the patient cannot. If he spontaneously and honestly conveys his thoughts and reactions, I believe he is not only communicating his concern, but he is in effect both eliciting and reinforcing kindred uncontrived behavior in his patient. To a shocking extent, behavior begets its own kind. Manipulation begets counter-manipulation. Real-self disclosure begets real-self disclosure. A therapist who *is* concerned about his patient's lot eventually will be perceived as a man of good will by his patient. Any man will hide his real self from those thought to be *not* of good will, just as a poker player hides his hand from the other players who are not of good will insofar as the player's money is concerned. In the presence of a man who *is* of good will, even the most defensive will strip themselves naked, such that the other will know their lot and be able to help them. Few women would submit to a medical examination if they thought the physician had voyeuristic motives rather than a desire to know their condition so as to be able to help them. No patient can be expected to drop all his defenses and reveal himself except in the presence of someone whom he believes is *for him,* and not for a theory, dogma, or technique. I believe that the therapist who abandons all attempts to shape his patient's behavior according to some predetermined scheme, and instead strives to know and to respond honestly to what he has learned, the therapist who aims at the establishment of a relationship of I and Thou, is doing his job as well as it can be done. That is, if spontaneous honesty between man and man and between a man and himself are worthwhile therapeutic goals. Somehow, I feel that *orthodox* therapists (we might call them Rogerian, Freudian, or even Skinnerian technicians) are more concerned to verify their respective dogmas than to know and respond to their patients as individual persons. Techniques treat with categories and fictions. Therapy proceeds through honest responses to this very person *by this very person.*

8

The Phenomenon of Resistance in the Psychotherapist*

One of Freud's monumental contributions to the art and science of psychotherapy was his discovery and elucidation of resistance and transference in the patient. As time went on, therapy came better to be understood as a dyadic transaction rather than as a monologue from the patient, with the person of the therapist hidden behind interpretations and the couch. One outcome of this realization was recognition of the countertransference. Today, most therapists are prepared to examine and reflect upon their own feelings and thoughts as they ebb and flow in the course of therapy.

But there is another phenomenon that arises in the therapist just as surely as it arises in the patient. I am referring now to what may be called *resistance to being* in the therapist. Just as a patient will pick and choose his utterances for their intended effect on the therapist (a violation of Freud's fundamental rule), so will a therapist often pick and choose his behavior for its supposed effect on the patient. This I now see as a violation of what may become a fundamental rule for the therapist: that he should be spontaneously open in response to the patient. Resistance to being, to being oneself with the patient, seems to be quite as characteristic of beginning therapists and of more experienced "technicians" of therapy as it is of patients and often for similar reasons, e.g., latent fear of how one will seem to the other as well as how one will seem to oneself, or dread of what will happen if one "lets go" of one's tight self-control.

In its starkest, most operational meaning, resistance in

---

* Adapted from a paper presented at the meeting of the Southeastern Psychological Association, Gatlinburg, Tennessee, April 14, 1961.

a patient refers to his reluctance or inability to disclose his thoughts, fantasies, feelings, or memories as these spontaneously arise in the therapeutic session. Rather than make himself known, the patient tries to manipulate his own disclosing behavior so as to shape the therapist's perceptions, feelings, and attitudes.

Just as the patient's ongoing stream of associations may be blocked by anxiety or picked over for some desired impact on the therapist, so may the therapist's utterances. The therapist may practice what Buber (1957, pp. 107-108) calls "semblance," or "seeming," as chronically as does the patient. This I suspect is inimical to growth of self in *both* parties. It has often happened that a patient has asked what I thought about him, or how I felt about him. Earlier, I would automatically reflect or restate his question or try to understand and then expound my opinion of his motives for asking. In technical terms, I was probably correct in responding to him in these ways, but I have now come to suspect that anxiety about disclosing to the patient what one thinks or feels about him may be one of the many forms of resistance to being and resistance to growth in the therapist, just as the patient's dread or inability to reveal his thoughts as they arise is resistance.

Hora (1960, pp. 498-499), speaking of existential psychotherapy, states, "The existential psychotherapist does not 'do' psychotherapy, *he lives it*. He meets his patient in the *openness* of an interhuman existential encounter. He does not seek to make interpretations, he does not evaluate and judge; *he allows what is to be, so that it can reveal itself in the essence of its being, and then proceeds to elucidate what he understands*."

In somewhat similar, but not identical vein, I have come gradually to see therapy, not as a setting in which one person, the therapist, *does things to a patient*, manipulating the relationship, the patient's behavior, or his own to make the patient get well or grow, but rather as a relationship that can be described in Buber's (1937) terminology—namely, an honest relationship gradually developing into one of I and Thou; a dialogue, in which growth of *both* parties is an outcome. I now suspect that the enforced discipline of making reflections or interpretations or even of "elucidating what he understands" (Hora, 1960) is behavior from the therapist that is not only of limited value to the patient, but is likewise confining for the therapist. An example will show what I mean by the latter: I have often found, following a number of therapeutic sessions, that I would be exhausted, and sometimes afflicted with a headache . . . symptoms that are common among people who have been forced to suppress or withhold spontaneous experience from disclosure in a face-to-face situation. Yet, as I reviewed the notes, or recording, or my memory of the sessions, I would discover that my behavior as a therapist had been technically faultless and had done the patient no harm. But I could also say in all honesty that my behavior had done no perceptible good either, for him or for me. I reasoned, "Surely behavior that does me harm can't be good for the patient." My technically correct behavior was in some sense defensive; and it seemed to impede my own growth as well as the patient's. I then wondered why I was so tense and exhausted. It soon became clear that my exhaustion came from withholding myself from my patient, from my own resistances to being, and I am now inclined to say, to growing.

With this realization, many recollections came rushing to me, of patients who had begged me to tell them what I thought, only to be met by my cool, faultless reflection or interpretation of their question, or else by a downright lie, e.g., "Yes, I like you," when in fact I found them boring or unlikable. Also, there came to me recollections of instances where I had violated what I thought were technical rules, for example, holding a weeping patient's hand, or bursting out laughing at something the patient had said, and of patients later telling me that when I had done those things, I somehow became human, a person, and that these were significant moments for the patients in the course of their therapy. Those of you who have read the recent *Critical Incidents in Psychotherapy* (Standal and Corsini, 1959) will see that in several of the instances cited (cf. pp. 30-39; 220-221; 233; 257) the therapist "broke through" his technical and character armor and responded in spontaneity to his patient.[1]

My behavior as a therapist has changed slowly, but radically, over the past couple of years. I am as good a listener as I ever was, perhaps better. My capacity for empathy and my over-all judgment are both greater now than they were earlier. I reflect feelings and content as I always did, but only when I want the patient to know what I heard him say. In fact, I agree with Rogers that there is no better way to tell a patient you heard him, and this acknowledged listening seems to reinforce further disclosing of *his* being from him. But I find myself sometimes giving advice, lecturing, laughing, becoming angry, interpreting, telling my fantasies, asking questions —in short, doing whatever occurs to me *during* the therapeutic session in response to the other person. This change could mean either that I am growing as a person and as a therapist, or else that, through lack of close supervision, I am losing in "discipline." Yet, I do discuss my work with colleagues, and I am not isolated.

My actual disclosures to the patient are still checked by common sense or by my judgment (I sometimes suspect that this is automatic and unconscious checking, though I realize this sounds mystical), but increasingly I find myself being more unpremeditated and spontaneous in my responses to the patient. It is as if I am coming more to trust myself, as if I trust that what comes out of me in response to a patient will not harm him or create a situation with which I cannot cope. This does not mean I am anti-intellectual, because I am not. Rather, it seems that, just as I can hear with a "third ear," I can sometimes listen to my "second voice"—the voice of my spontaneous response. Perhaps here we have the active counterpart to Theodore Reik's classic, *Listening with the Third Ear*, namely, "Speaking with the Second Voice." [2]

[1] I cannot help but comment, though, that we have no published record that I know of, of instances where spontaneous being from the therapist had done real harm to the relationship, the patient, and the therapist.

[2] If spontaneous disclosure occurs, developmentally, *before*

When I become strictly technical and hence impersonal with my patients, I have learned it is usually because I have become anxious. When I am lucky enough
to recognize my anxiety, I will sometimes say, "You are
making me anxious." If I am angry, I let this be known.
If I am concerned or worried, I let this be known.

If a patient asks me a question that I genuinely would
rather not answer, I tell him, "I'd rather not answer."
I give him true reasons, too. The most succinct way I
have of describing what I do is that I strive to give the
patient an openness of myself in that moment. I believe
that he is entitled to an honest expression of myself as
a professional man, and this is what I give him. This is
the transparency, the "congruence," which Rogers (1961)
has so lucidly described. He states (Rogers, 1961, pp.
5-7), for example, "congruence is the opposite of pre-
senting a façade, a defensive front, to the patient or
client. If the therapist is experiencing one thing in the
relationship, but is endeavoring to be something else,
then the condition (of congruence) is not met. . . ."
"To be transparent to the client, to have nothing of
one's experience in the *relationship* which is hidden . . .
this is, I believe, basic to effective psychotherapy. . . .
The therapist, by being openly and freely himself, is
ready for and is offering the possibility of an existential
encounter between two real persons. . . . (It) is these
moments, I believe, which are therapeutic."

Buber, in speaking of "genuine dialogue," states
(1957, pp. 112-113) that ". . . if genuine dialogue is to
arise, everyone who takes part in it must bring himself
into it. . . . He must be willing on each occasion to say
what is really in his mind about the subject of the conversation. . . . No one . . . *can know in advance what
it is that he has to say*."

The question then arises, why not be thus spontaneous
and open? There are many objections that come to mind.
One grows from what I believe *is the assumption that
it is technique as such which promotes growth or well-*

---

contrived disclosure, then it might be more accurate to regard
technical responses from a therapist as the "second voice,"
and spontaneous utterance as the "first."

ness in a patient, and there is really no evidence I know of to support such an assumption, unless it lies in the data which deals with the placebo effect (Shapiro, 1960). Doubtless technical behavior impresses patients who are impressible by such "magic"—and we should not lightly dismiss the value of magic. We still do not understand the psychological and neurological mechanisms of faith, hope, and *charisma!* Fiedler's (1950) studies and Eysenck's (1952) cast grave doubt on the healing powers of technique *per se*. Technique, including reflection, silence, interpretation, seems to function as a defense against immature being, and it is doubtless valuable for that reason. Furthermore, it is often a safe or harmless way to interact and hence has value for that purpose. Finally, technique can be taught.

Another objection to openness is that therapists may fear that in being their real selves in the therapeutic session they may harm the patient, or "act out" in various ways. Or they may reveal their immaturity or ineptitude. The patient may then stop and go elsewhere for help —not such a bad thing after all, if he is not getting understanding and growth-yielding behavior from the therapist. I don't think expert technique can long hide immaturity, anxiety, hostility, sexuality, if these exist in the therapist. Patients are seldom that insensitive. Moreover, if a therapist thus hides his being, he is engaging in the same behavior that generated symptoms in the patient, and supposedly, he is trying to undo this self-alienating process.

The spontaneous dialogue in which a therapist can engage with his patients (if he dares) seems to result in the outcomes that the patient will come to know him as *he is during the hours together*. (One need not tell the patient about one's life outside the therapy hour, unless one wishes.) This serves, among other things, gradually to correct the patient's transference misperceptions as they arise. Furthermore, spontaneity makes the therapist's responses unpredictable and uncontrollable by the patient. (Evidently, it is only the therapist's good will that needs to be assured and predictable, not his actual verbal responses.) This tends to "up-end" many of his expectancies, in Frank Shaw's (1957) terms, and also to help extinguish omnipotence fantasies that arise in chronic manipulators.

Another outcome is that the therapist's openness serves gradually to relieve the patient's distrust, something which most patients bring with them into therapy. Still another outcome is that the therapist, by being open, by letting himself be as well as he lets the patient be (cf. Hora, 1960), provides the patient with a role-model of growth-yielding interpersonal behavior with which he can identify. Many a patient has ended orthodox psychoanalytic, or client-centered, therapy as a good listener, as a reflector of feelings or a dispenser of theoretically sound interpretations of his own or other's behavior, but such persons seldom make themselves very popular. Not that popularity is a desired outcome to therapy. But they have acquired these traits through mimicry, through identification with the behavior of their therapists. Since identification does occur, we may as well provide a wholesome, wellness-conducive model. As Jung says (1933, p. 51), "Be the man through whom you wish to influence others." Whitehorn (1959, p. 5) too has called attention to the leadership function of the therapist, and we know that good leaders provide good examples or role-models to their followers.

Spontaneous disclosure by the therapist of his ongoing inner experience during a session does not mean that therapists should stop using technique, making diagnoses, or using judgment, but rather that they will frequently think out loud, or else tell the patient frankly that they do not want to express their thinking right now.

Some Signs of Resistance in the Therapist

1. Having fantasies during the session, and not disclosing them.
2. Giving chronically technical responses rather than spontaneous responses.
3. Lying to the patient about one's opinions, attitudes, or feelings.
4. Withholding expressions of like, dislike, boredom, irritation.

Proof, of course, is required to support the hypothesis that an I-Thou relationship, marked by unreserve in both parties, is the means and the goal of therapy. But review of existing studies (Eysenck, 1952; Fiedler, 1950) and opinions (Jung, 1933; Rogers, 1961) seems to point to the hypothesis that resistance to being in the therapist is a deterrent to growth of being in the patient.

Another implication of *being* in the therapist seems to be this: that a therapeutic relationship can change the therapist as much as it does the patient. This means that those who wish to leave their being and their growth unchanged should not become therapists.

It would seem that we can propose a hypothesis that could be tested, namely, that spontaneous real-self being in a therapist reinforces, or is a condition for, real-self being and growth in the patient, while impersonality, technical behavior, and resistance to being reinforces the like in the patient.[3] I believe therapists could judge their own protocols for examples of such behavior and then explore relationships between such behavior and the subsequent behavior of the patient.

The question may properly be raised, "What is so good, or therapeutic, about a qualified therapist's spontaneity in his relationships with his patient? Why should it promote growth and wellness in patients, when the spontaneous behavior of the patient's family and friends has *not* produced these outcomes?" Indeed, the spontaneous responses of the patient's family and friends may have contributed to the development of pathology in the patient.

[3] Leonard Krasner, a brilliant researcher in the operant conditioning of verbal behavior, wrote me thus: ". . . it may very well be that research will indicate that the most effective therapists 'are themselves' in their relationship with the patient. However, I would feel that the therapist acting 'spontaneously' still represents a person who has been highly 'programmed' via his training, schooling, and previous interpersonal contacts. Probably the most effective way to 'control' another person's behavior is to 'be spontaneous' in the relationship with them. Of course, what I am suggesting is that there is no such thing as spontaneity. Anyway, we can probably get into a good controversy on this" (Personal Correspondence, April 11, 1961).

For a full elucidation of Krasner's views, see Krasner, L. The Therapist as a Social Reinforcement Machine. In Strupp, H. H., and Luborsky, L., *Research in Psychotherapy*, Vol. II, American Psychological Association, Washington, D.C., 1962, pp. 61-94.

A tentative answer to these questions would seem to be that the therapist, first of all, has a broader and deeper perspective on the dynamics of behavior than laymen would have. Second, he will not be so readily threatened by the patient's pathology or by the patient's growth. Third, the therapist is "set," or oriented toward the promotion of growth and fuller functioning, whereas family and friends of the patient may, without their awareness, be subtly reinforcing the patient's pathology and impeding his efforts to grow. Finally, but not least in importance, the setting in which therapy usually is transacted is one which fosters full self-disclosure from the patient and attentive listening in the therapist. To be really heard is a rarity in everyday life.

Another question that arises is this: Is the spontaneity of a trained therapist of a different kind and quality and effect from the spontaneity of a beginning therapist who has not yet even become the master of his techniques? My supposition is that the spontaneity that transcends technique is different from beginners' spontaneity, different because of the fact that the therapist has been through a disciplined training program. Among other things, the discipline in technique introduces the beginning therapist to a mode of relating to others that is different from the modes he learned as he was socialized; it is a sort of weaning from previously unexamined patterns of interpersonal behavior. *What seems called for in most training programs, however, is encouragement and direction in modes of transcending or abandoning self-conscious or automatized technique in relating to patients.* Many therapists come to feel guilty when their own growth makes their techniques seem restrictive, and when they impulsively respond to a patient at a real-self level. Those of us who train psychotherapists have much to learn from Zen masters in the art of eliciting unpremeditated behavior from our well-indoctrinated pupils.

Perhaps these comments about resistance to being in the therapist belong most properly to the later stages of therapy, those that lie beyond what Jung (1933) spoke of as the stage of confession. Jung divided the therapeutic process into a stage of confession, a stage of explanation, a stage of education, and finally, a stage of transformation. Possibly technique, such as reflection and interpretation, or even "reinforcement," brings a patient through the stages of confession and explanation, but leaves the therapist untouched and unresponsive as a person. If therapy is to proceed through the stages of education and transformation, resistance to being in the therapist must be overcome, and he must interact and grow with his patient.

Part IV

Role of "Inspiritation" in Wellness

9

The Role of Spirit and "Inspiriting" in Human Wellness

It is to be expected that scientists will deal only with realities and not with the figments of poetic or religious fancy. "Spirit," because of its fanciful implications, has largely been banished from the realms of science and even metaphysics. It implies a dualistic conception of reality, and dualisms present irreconcilable impasses to the scientist.

Yet, I am beginning to believe, on the basis of much evidence, hitherto scattered and from apparently unrelated realms, that *something* in the human organism functions in the manner that poets and preachers have said the soul and spirit function. For the time being, I will include the term "spirit" in my scientific vocabulary and define it operationally, or try to.

Let me first assert that the human organism represents an organization of tissues, cells, and so forth which constitute a *system* (cf. Miller, 1955). In any system the modes of functioning (output) and even the structural limits of any given part are confined to some range by restrictions imposed by the system as a whole, and of course the given part plays a similar role in defining the limits and output of other parts and the system as a whole. The main output of the human organism, considered as a whole, is behavior. This output, *behavior*, affects the system and is affected by the system.

Now, let us postulate that the system as a whole can be characterized as efficient or inefficient. The former mode of organization mediates valued output from the whole system and yet preserves the integrity of the system against forces of dissolution. "Inefficient" organization, by contrast, results in defective output or output at the cost of the integrity of the system, or both. Inefficiently organized systems have low resistance to the "forces of entropy" which, for the human, include proliferation of germs and bacteria, stress-effects, runaway growth of cells, etc.

"Spirit" will be said to be maximal when the organization of the system is optimum, mediating valued and effective behavioral output. At the time organization is optimum, the human person is characterized subjectively by such states as *absorbing interest,* intense *commitment* to some goal or value, faith in God, the doctor, medicine, the strength of his body, love, prayer, or almost anything. Perhaps one of these states is a necessary condition for optimum organization and output. It is possible that this subjective phenomenon is isomorphic to some pattern of brain functioning which "inspirits" the body-system as a whole, thus maximally resisting entropy.

Some assumption such as that of "spirit" and "inspiriting" is necessary to account for a broad range of phenomena presently not understood, though reliably observed. In order to abet subsequent discussion, let me postulate an imaginary (but with possible empirical referents) *spirit-titre.*

SPIRIT-TITRE

Let us visualize spirit-titre as varying from zero to 100. At zero, death and dissolution of the body have 100 per cent probability. A level of 100 is likely an heuristic limit that can be approached but not reached, or if reached, cannot be sustained for more than a few moments duration—as in the peak experiences which Maslow (1961) describes. Probably, most "normal" people (that is, people who live a life of modal, respectable, socially patterned behavior) could be characterized as possessing a spirit-titre somewhere between the range of 30 to 60, with a mode of 45. Let us assert that at this level, modal behavior is possible, but the body-system is not overly resistant to the ubiquitous germs, viruses, or effects of stress that are the inexorable consequence of the very way of life that is called "respectability." Consequently, it could be said, with near certainty, that "normal" behavior—behavior conforming with the usual age, sex, and occupational roles—regularly yields: (a) social acceptability, or at least avoidance of moral or legal condemnation; (b) status-defense or enhancement; (c) minimal gratification of body-system "needs" (which results in rudimentary increases in spirit-titre); and (d) recurrent illness as we presently define illness.

When spirit-titre falls below some wellness-sustaining level—say around 20 or 30 units—the person is characterized subjectively by "low spirits," depression, boredom, diffuse anxiety, or kindred dysphoric psychological states. Simultaneous with the psychological state of affairs, it might be observed that the elegance, precision, and zeal of the person's behavioral output has diminished. Doubtless, in time, the low spirit-titre permits "illness" to take root; microbes or viruses multiply, stress-by-products proliferate, "latent" illnesses become manifest or "galloping."

It is a reliable medical and pharmacologic observation that when people are "sick" every transaction which the patient carries on with a person, drug, God, chiropractor, or Christian Science practitioner—indeed, whatever inspires *faith*—has "beneficial" effects, even under so-called double-blind conditions. The "placebo-effect" is inevitable (Shapiro, 1960), however troublesome it may be to the pharmacologist interested in controlling it or canceling it so as to specify the "pure" effect of a drug on a tissue or a system.

I would like to propose again as a "new discovery" what every physician is taught and comes to know through his studies in physiology: that "healing" is rooted in the body-system and that at best the therapists co-operate with "Nature." *They* do not cure, nor do their medicines or surgical procedures. Probably the *confidence* which the patient has in the physician (or in the witch-doctor, chiropractor, or in Lydia Pinkham) is the signal, trigger, occasion, or the psychological manifestation of the self-healing "spirit" which welds the body-system into its optimum illness-combating and illness-resisting organization.

In short, medical *expertise* has the significance of constituting an "injection," or more properly an occasion for release of spirit which increases the patient's spirit-titre to the wellness-mediating range. This is not to deny that some medical procedures involving drugs and surgery do have non-spiritual effects. Perhaps antibiotics and surgery, for example, function much like poison or a .22 rifle in a campaign to reduce the number of mice, which has multiplied following the removal of natural mice-predators in a given ecological niche. If a farm, say, can function and produce an optimal output only when there are between 300 and 1000 mice in the barn; and when there are no owls around, and 6 of the farmer's 10 cats have died, then poisoning or shooting some of the mice may reduce their numbers to the point where 4 cats can keep their number to the optimum range. Incidentally, it may well be that the field of "intra-body ecology" has barely been scratched.

Let us now ask the question, what inspirits a person? What will function so as to increase a person's spirit-titre from the lower to the higher reaches?

INSPIRITATION—SPIRIT-MOBILIZATION—AT VARIOUS SPIRIT-TITRE LEVELS

Let us begin this discussion by considering the problem of inspiritation at the lower levels, when a person is sick, even unto dying. In our culture, such persons are generally to be found under medical care, in or out of hospitals. We can ask, of course, what was the modal spirit-level of these people during the time prior to their present low level of spirit. But let us take them as we find them, and see what the typical course of events might be. First of all, the patient is usually now away from a dispiriting, sickness-yielding milieu, and this change of milieu can have inspiriting consequences by itself. Second, he has placed himself in the hands of specialists whom he has been trained to trust. This is notoriously inspiriting. Third, he is looked at, poked, probed, punctured, diagnosed, dosed, cut open—all of which have both specific situational consequences and also a general inspiriting effect. In analogy with Selye's (1950) formulations (he showed that any stressor both has specific noxious effects and sets in motion a more or less stereotyped "general adaptation syndrome") the entire medical armamentorium produces specific, local beneficent effects, but possibly too it sets in motion a *general hope syndrome*. This may be characterized as a gradually rising titre of spirit which in turn decreases the entropic level of the body-system; that is, it mediates higher-level wellness. When the spirit-titre rises, entropy decreases, and the person's body again is characterized by a spirit-titre that mediates "normal" behavior and that often "throws off" symptoms for a time. When the dispiriting forces recur, however, the spirit-titre drops and symptoms recur, which perhaps explains why new therapies and even placebos have only temporary effectiveness.

Sometimes, a patient has no hope, nothing to live for; he has "given up"; his "spirits fall" to a low ebb. When this is observed to happen, of course, a dismal prognosis is indicated. Yet, the history of medicine is replete with examples of "miraculous" recoveries from fatal illness and tissue-destruction, where the miracle consisted in a recovery by the patient of the will to live, the discovery that life was worth living, the discovery that people care, that they were praying for his recovery (Arthur Godfrey acknowledged with thanks the prayers which *he knew* were being offered in his behalf, and in which possibly he had confidence). By the same token, less seriously ill people have had their symptoms remitted by "placebos" in which they had faith and confidence, through "suggestion." It may be suggested, then, that all healing is faith-healing, in the sense that the patient has faith in what is being done to heal him. This faith triggers off an increase in spirit-titre; the increasing spirit-titre is the signal that healing is going on.

Oddly enough, the people who respond to drug placebos are often regarded or adjudged to be morally inferior, suggestible people who are not even "really" sick. People who get well in response to powerful drug agents somehow are deemed really sick. I see no reason for us to assume that the person who gets well following a drug placebo is any the less sick than someone who responds only to "true medicine." In a way, the placebo-responder may be a luckier person; no matter why he gets sick, his powers of self-healing can be mobilized by substances that are harmless to his organism, whereas the more medically sophisticated have to be dosed with substances that might have directly injurious effects. Possibly, too, the people who respond to powerful medicines are really only highly suspicious people whose spirit and faith has been conditioned, not to the good will of their fellow man, or to pink sugar-pills, but only to dangerous drugs.

Conditioning the Spirit

If a man's spirit-titre, or his spirit-response, is conditionable, as there seems reason to suspect, then an entire new field opens for investigation. Psychotherapists, physicians, quacks, witch-doctors all can attest that confidence of the patient in the "powers" of the healer must be inspired if the healing rituals are to work. They do not hesitate to use all manner of symbols that in many instances serve as conditioned stimuli evoking the faith-response, which truly does the healing. A good question for us to ask is, what is the unconditioned, primitive stimulus or stimuli which evoke faith, confidence, or an increase in spirit-titre? Possibly any experience that induces richer satisfactions in living, that reduces anxiety and permits successful, coping behavior to emerge. Possibly the assurance of a mother or a father, mediated by cuddling, hugging, or other symbols of protection, care, or effort on one's own behalf, inspire faith and surges of spirit. We need to discover some empirical response which would permit us to study a sample of spirit by the techniques of the conditioning laboratory.

Spirit and Aging

Let us next consider the phenomenon of collapse, or demoralization, which commonly follows male retirement from productive work. For many men, their spirit-titre has become (through training) conditioned to a certain delimited mode of life, namely, the pursuit, through work, of money, status, or prestige. Their very sense of identity (is this a psychological counterpart of spirit?) is rooted in their occupational role. When this has been taken away through forcible retirement, it can produce "demoralization"—being at a loss as to what, of personal value, the individual can do with himself. Under such conditions, depression—loss of spirit—is common, as is the onset of assorted physical and/or psychiatric conditions. It is interesting that women live longer than men, though this mortality differential has not as yet been fully explained. I wonder whether the woman's *role*, in our society at least, does not permit her *to be herself*, her womanly self, even into her 90's, by the simple expedient of training and permitting her to knit, sew, clean, and look after spouse, children, and grandchildren so long as she has a breath in her body. She maintains a lively and concerned interest in the personal affairs of her loved ones. These things—meaningful work, and loving, spirited concern—are doubtless inspiriting, and keep the older woman's body as anti-entropic as her aging tissues permit.

The modal male, on the other hand, cannot consider himself "manly" by doing trivial things, and he cannot be so "womanly" as to "snoop into the private affairs of others." Doubtless, then, man's spiritual titre drops lower and lower, until he dies—several years before his female compeer. Yet, we can also observe many older men who have been "prepared" for retirement, or who have maintained some lively interests, or who have important (to them and to society) work which "gives them something to live for"—it keeps their spirit-titre maximal. One thinks of Freud, who lived the last 15 years or so of his life with a mouth cancer. One wonders whether it was just a "weak" cancer, or whether his spirit-level was sufficiently high to so mobilize his body that it contained the cancerous growth within limits that permitted him to continue productive work. The 100-year-old vegetating Civil War generals doubtless had their spirits kept up to the level which sustained life because they felt *their continued existence was wanted and needed*, if for no other reason than that of satisfying the museum-passions of the larger population. I wonder, too, whether men in their 70's or 80's who have been obliged to assume "womanly" work—as in taking care of a bed-ridden wife of kindred age—whether such men are not inspirited, no matter how much they may resent or loathe the work. At least the needs of the helpless partner give them something useful to which they can devote even feeble powers of locomotion, vision for reading, tremulous manual skills for feeding and cleaning, etc. One wonders too whether women who have abandoned much of the traditional woman's role, and have become professionals, or business-careerists—whether their illness patterns and mean life expectancy are not more similar to that of the modal male.

Spirit and Normal Personality

Let us now consider inspiritation at levels somewhat above those found in the frankly ill. I should like to propose that the so-called normal, "adjusted" person in our society lives a mode of life or behaves typically in ways that keep his spirit-titre considerably below the upper limit. If the upper limit is 100, and a spirit-titre of 30 permits illness to emerge, then perhaps "normal" people function somewhere between about 35 and 55. What this means subjectively is that they seldom know great joy, great enthusiasm, passionate dedication; they seldom function in ways which unfold their productive potential; in terms of sheer work-output, they seldom produce much. An intriguing observation is that noted in the now-classic Hawthorne study in industrial psychology (Roethlisberger and Dickson, 1939). Investigators wanted to study the effect of various environmental manipulations on the work output of female workers in a telephone factory. In the crucial test, one group was subjected to brighter illumination in their workroom, while a control group had dimmer lighting. Work output and morale increased in *both groups*. It would seem that merely being singled out as important enough to be studied removed the *dispiriting* effect of anonymity and impersonality, and resulted in an increase in spirit-titre, which in turn facilitated more output. The many subsequent studies of factors in "morale" in military and work situations can readily be interpreted as studies of factors which increase spirit-titre.

Thus, in the so-called "normal" person, the one who is not sick, higher-level (beyond normality) wellness appears to ensue from such events as having one's individuality respected and acknowledged—hence the often beneficial effects of simple, nondirective counseling, i.e., of being listened to with understanding. It seems to reinforce identity, mobilize spirit, and promote self-healing.

Being the recipient of love from another appears to be a highly inspiriting event. There have been many informal observations of people, previously limp, lack-luster, dispirited people, who increased in zeal, muscle tonus, integration of personality, and in resistance to illness, once they were told they were loved by some significant other person.

At the higher levels of wellness, inspiritation appears to make it possible for a person to actualize all manner of potentialities for valued output. An "inspiring" teacher isn't necessarily a pedagogue well-schooled in the "latest teaching methods." Rather, the inspiring teacher appears to be a person who mobilizes higher levels of spirit in the pupil, which in turn mediates more focused and effective utilization of energies and problem-solving abilities. Assuming that rudimentary "health habits" are observed, it is doubtless true that more highly inspirited people become ill less often than less-spirited people. People with much to live for, who love deeply and broadly and draw on their inner resources to solve the mysteries of the universe and to satisfy the needs and wants of mankind, probably live longer than less dedicated people. Sorokin (1958) found, in a study of "saints" throughout history, that their life span, characterized by "good works," was longer than the mean.

What about *reduction* of spirit in the "normal" person? It is known that at least among primitive societies, people will die when they have been banished from the tribe, or when they have learned that a witch-doctor has put a hex on them. This probably diminishes spirit-titre to a very low ebb indeed, permitting entropy to maximize.

There is doubtless, too, a class of dispiriting people who maintain their own spirit-level by functioning among others so as to demoralize them, to undermine their faith and confidence in themselves, who literally produce a pain in the neck of the people with whom they come in contact. The comic character, "Joe Btfisk," in "L'il Abner," with his little black cloud following him everywhere, spreads entropy wherever he goes. Superb pianists cannot play a note when he is near, hens don't lay, sick people get sicker. The Yiddish "yenta" and "qvetch" are doubtless similar spirit-droppers and fomenters of the slow heal and galloping disorganization. So too is Stephen Potter's (1952) "one-upman." One wonders if the life-principle which Freud called "eros," in contrast with "thanatos," does not refer to the spirit which we have been talking about.

What, in general, may be regarded as events which sustain or increase a given spirit-titre? Probably all instances of behavior which yield rich satisfaction of needs at all levels ranging from physical needs to "self-actualizing" experiences. Thus, a successful outcome to a challenging task is probably inspiriting. So too is a richly gratifying, loving sexual experience. So too is the receipt of honest and spontaneous praise, acceptance, or endorsement. Having one's individuality accepted, honored, and acknowledged is likely inspiriting, just as removal of personal identity can be dispiriting. The offer of help, with no strings attached, when one's spirit is "low" is likely an inspiriting experience. We need data on this. Possibly introspective reports and physiological measures of all kinds might be correlated with life situations to yield a research footing into the realm of spirit.

"Mental Illness" and Spirit-Titre

A given culture offers its denizens a design for living that includes valued goals and specification of means for reaching these goals. Many of the mentally ill may be regarded as people who have "given up" the race for culturally meaningful symbols of success. Their spirit-titre has dropped below the level which mediates "healthy behavior." Thus, a given culture may require people to avoid behavior which, if engaged in, might yield rich gratification. Or, a given social milieu may be so devoid of opportunities for inspiriting satisfactions of "love" needs, security needs, esteem needs, sexual needs, etc., that the person becomes demoralized, or dispirited. It is probably possible to assess the spirit-mobilizing or spirit-level-maintaining qualities of a given social structure or a given cultural pattern for living.

Psychotherapy, the deliberate attempt to modify a person's behavior from the range which produces and perpetuates "symptoms" to a pattern that is both socially acceptable and inspiriting, has not yet been placed on a scientific basis. By this is meant the fact that no one theory of psychotherapy has been proven "right" while conflicting theories are proven wrong. Instead, accumulating evidence points to a "placebo effect" even in psychotherapy (Rosenthal and Frank, 1956): those patients are maximally helped by a given regime of psychotherapy who have faith that this technique or this particular practitioner will be of avail to them in their quest for fuller functioning. The fact was noted above that a person who responds to placebos, a "suggestible" person, is regarded tacitly by physicians and psychologists as a kind of second-rate citizen. It is curious because, when we re-examine the "placebo effect," it amounts to the mobilization of spirit in a person such that his body and personality come to be more efficiently organized against disintegration. This mobilization is accomplished, not through pharmaceutical means, but rather through the impact of man on man, mediated through the patient's perceptual-cognitive structure. In short, the interpretation of events (probably a brain phenomenon) is seen to have killing and healing properties which have been observed (Christenson, Kane, Wolff, and Hinkle, 1958), but have remained largely unplumbed by scientists, though the power of the subjective interpretation has been exploited by primitive witch-doctors, as well as by "quacks" and "charlatans" in our society.

Practical and Theoretical Implications of Spirit and Inspiration

Obviously, we need to understand more about spirit, its dimensions and conditions. It would be most helpful if we could devise indices that would permit estimation of this hypothetical spirit-titre that we have spoken of so glibly. Possibly, neurophysiologists may, at some time, be able to specify the locus of spirit in the brain—and I do not mean a re-activation of the old quest for the site of the soul, as in Descartes' day and earlier.

Practically, there is much to be said for learning the art of inspiration not only in everyday interpersonal transactions, but also in such professions as medicine, nursing, teaching, and the psychotherapeutic arts. We have, I think, capitalized informally on the "magic" of faith, confidence, prayer, placebos, and so on, but without taking the phenomenon seriously enough as a natural event that warrants study. If it be true, as some psychoanalysts maintain, that God is a symbol of man's never-reached ultimate powers, and that man has denied or become alienated from his powers, then if prayer and worship are effective in helping a man re-own these powers, we ought to learn more about prayer. If man's powers of healing are rooted in his body, but man doesn't know this, and believes instead that the power of healing is "out there," in the physician's black bag, then displaying the black bag perhaps is *not* the most effective way of mobilizing man's self-healing power, or spirit. I think that once we begin seriously to study "spirit" as a natural phenomenon,[1] we will not only increase our grasp of nature's laws, but we will radically alter many of our practical pursuits.

[1] See Chapter 18 for some suggested ways to approach the study of spirit.

10

Body Image, Spirit, and Wellness*

In America any woman of any age whose bodily measures are not 36-24-35 feels low in spirits. Although I have never interviewed one, I believe it might be found that a Bushman lady with hip measurements of less than 50 inches (they run to steatopygia there, and according to anthropological accounts they like it) might likewise become dispirited.

In our society, a body image among men and women is a work of art, an embellishment or camouflage of endowment and diet. When one's body is disliked because of deviation from norms for function or appearance, replicated evidence shows that anxiety, insecurity, and low self-esteem are regular correlates.

Now, you may notice that I used some terms above that are rather in disrepute among hard-headed psychologists, namely "low in spirits" and "dispirited." Let me ask you to reconsider some of these terms with me.

A nagging and persistent problem to psychologists *is* spirit. For centuries, nonscientific man has insisted that the spirit is real and that it is the essential part, the truly human part of man. Hard-headed empiricists banish the spirit to limbo time and again, with good reason, and yet the artist, the minister, the layman all have hung on to this and cognate concepts. Personally, I think many psychologists read and listen to each other too much and do not pay enough attention to what humanists have noticed about man through the ages. I, for one, have gotten interested lately in taking a fresh look at the concept of spirit in particular, and, following the procedure which Fritz Heider (1958) calls "naïve psychology," I have begun to look at what is *there* that is observable and describable when people say "He is a spir-

* Presented at the American Psychological Association meeting, September, 1959, Cincinnati, Ohio, on the symposium "A Body-Image Approach to Behavior."

ited lad"; "Her spirit is broken"; "His spirits fell"; and so on. Truly, I have found this new "spiritualism" refreshing, and what is rare in psychology, exciting.

My assignment on the symposium was to deliver a paper on Body-Image and Cultural Norms. My title and my talk may seem remote from that assignment at this point, but as it proceeds, you will see, I hope, that it is not so really far removed. To anticipate what follows, I think that the body image, if that is indeed what Fisher and Cleveland have been measuring with their ingenious "Penetration" and "Barrier" scores, may well be a very important indicant of the nature and quality of the organization of that system, man-in-milieu. It may, in short, be an index of what I have chosen thus far to call spirit-titre.

Now, when a person is said to have high spirits, or to be enthused, or inspirited, he likely might also be described as active, expressive, effective in his behavior, and of high morale. Probably, when a person says he is in high spirits, or feeling good, there are physical, chemical, and neural concomitants to that state. Doubtless, too, there are external, describable conditions that are necessary and sufficient to produce a "high-spirit" response—for example, being told that some significant other loves you, or being engaged in effort toward personally worthwhile goals with high expectation of success.

I propose to recall our attention to this mode of being which might be called highly inspirited and about which we likely have already learned a good deal in other contexts. I will propose some new terms and use some old ones, such as spirit-titre, hope, the general hope syndrome, spirit-responses, and spirit-center, and then try to relate such concepts to my assigned topic on this symposium.

First, spirit-titre. Let us postulate that man, regarded as a *system* (call it the person-body-milieu system), can assume modes of organization of the parts which are optimum and maximally efficient both for the mediation of valued behavior and for maintenance of the integrity of the system itself. He can also assume modes of organization which sacrifice either output or the integrity of the system, or both. Let me suggest that maximum spirit-titre is illustrated by those states when the system is optimally organized. Minimum spirit-titre is manifest when man's system is so organized that it yields either the minimum of valued behavioral output or output at the cost of pain or disease, or both.

When spirit-titre is maximum, the system as a whole is maximally resistant to the omnipresent forces of entropy which, unchecked, would ensure that man would assume his most probable state under the sun, namely, some chemicals organized in a state not recognizable as man. At the time spirit-titre, thus defined, is optimum, man is probably characterized by a momentary integration of his self-structure and engaged in a personally worth-while mission or goal in life which polarizes his energy-output; in short, he is *committed to life*. These subjective states, discoverable only through study and interpretation of a person's self-disclosures, are *conditions* or signs, or both, of the optimum organization of the system for enduring and behaving at the higher levels of wellness.

Now, if we just look about us at man in the average, at "normal" man, we can assert that he seldom achieves the higher spirit-titres. Most normal men fall ill a few times a year, and following rest or treatment, their system returns to a mode of organization which is not much more resistant to entropy, or disorganization, than it was before the illness. In fact, when ill, a man may recover, or find relief from pain, following treatments which have little pharmacologic rationale. Placebos, for example, are sometimes as effective in abetting cure of illness or relief from pain as are powerful drugs or radical surgery. Studies of the placebo-effect have strongly suggested that *faith* in the therapy or the therapist may well be *the* force that abets healing. We know that healing is rooted in the organism, not in the pill, hypodermic, or scalpel, although we and physicians often forget this fact, despite endless discussion of homeostasis. It has also been long noted that if a sick person *has no will to live*, or nothing to live for, his prognosis may well be dismal, in spite of excellent and aseptic medical care. Considerations such as these have led me to postulate a *general hope syndrome* which is set in motion when a sick person is subjected to some treatment—even such as Borgatta's (1959) "Limbotherapy"—that inspires hope. Any treatment has local and specific effects, like a scratch on the skin following injection of saline solution, but it will have a more general, stereotyped effect analogous with Selye's (1950) general adaptation syndrome—it will result in the reorganization of the *system* such that the system then affords a milieu that is highly uncongenial for cancer-growth, bacteria and virus proliferation, and the corrosive effects of stress byproducts. This reorganization, in turn, ultimately results in, or *is*, the re-establishment of "health." In short, it may be true that specific drug and surgical therapy, even psychotherapy, are all, in the last analysis, faith-healing. Those procedures heal people who have faith in such procedures. Loving care, in which someone has faith and confidence, induces *hope*, which in turn is a manifestation, concomitant, or cause of inspiration—a gain in spirit-titre.

Nursing has much to teach us here, both about the art of inspiration and about body-image correlates of spirit. Grooming patients, for example, seems to affect recovery from mental and physical illness. Let me call our attention to some cognate phenomena. It is a common observation in any organized group that when "morale" is low, productivity is minimal, and illness becomes common. When the group is well led, and when the members feel that it is devoted to worth-while goals, output increases, and illness among the members often decreases or vanishes. Could it be, then, that there are some modes of social organization which abet maximal spirit-titre and others which actively reduce the level of spirit—the mode of intra-person organization—to that pattern which will not permit either valued output or wellness to emerge or endure? Are there cultures and groups that sicken or kill their members young? Medical ecologists and sociologists assure us that this is true.

Consider even a group of two people. We have ample reason to suspect that there are persons who, like Joe Btfisk in "L'il Abner," have a black cloud as a constant companion and spread chaos and entropy wherever they go. Hens don't lay, pianists cannot perform, golfers cannot drive. Stephen Potter's schools of one-upmanship, lifemanship, and gamesmanship likely graduate many such dispiriting characters.

Now, I direct our attention to the phenomena of differential longevity. Commonly, it is observed that many men in our culture who are not "prepared" for retirement languish and die soon after they have gone on a pension. It may be that they die of boredom; or, in our present jargon, they die because they withdraw from work which sustains their identity and gives them something to use themselves for. This withdrawal results in a reduction of spirit-titre, such that cancer or other latent illness runs away. "Host-resistance" may be fostered by a goal or mission in life and diminished when such is removed. It is even possible that the statement, "I am old, or you are old, and hence all washed up," if believed, can result in a change in the organization of a person's intra-body ecology such that natural predators of germs and systemic defenses against cancerous growth are no longer adequate to sustain wellness. Such a self-conception may even be reflected in the body-image concepts as manifested in Rorschach responses. We know too that women live longer than men in our society, and it may well be because the woman's role, as culturally defined, permits them to find something useful to do, even when very old. Women can't retire from cleaning, or from lively, or "nosy" interest in the affairs of others. Women, for that matter, are inspirited or dispirited by their appearance, as both research and charm school attest. Positive body-cathexis is likely inspiriting.

Next let us look at voodoo death. Anthropologists have long been aware of the fact that in primitive societies a man may die when *he learns* he has broken a taboo or learns that the medicine man is working magic in order to hasten his demise. The man may die either of shock or because his spirit-titre has diminished to the point that vital functions cannot continue. He dies then of some proximate cause mainly because he has no particular hope or expectation of further living. He may even be slain by some animal that previously he was sufficiently well-organized, or inspirited, to outwit and destroy.

Observers in concentration camps during World War

II pointed out that chances for surviving the incredibly stressing conditions of existence were enhanced when a person had a firm grip on some reason for surviving, such as hatred of the enemy, or profound love of another person. These examples serve only to highlight the importance of a goal in life, one that is worth-while for the person, as a factor which mobilizes spirit or organizes the body such that it sustains life and mediates effective behavioral output.

Now, these examples *may* make it possible for us to postulate a spirit-center (is the reticular formation the new seat or site of the soul?) in some central locus, which mediates what I will call the spirit-response—the progressive, orderly change in organization of the person-body-milieu system from one that is relatively inefficient to sustain integrity or wellness and valued output, to a more efficient pattern of organization. It is probably the spirit-response which sets the general hope syndrome in motion. It is probably the spirit-response which is mobilized by any event that signifies hope or confidence in self or in the future; it is probably the spirit-response which, when weakened, permits illness to flourish.

If there is a spirit-response, if this is not mere word-play, it could well be that it functions like any conditioned response. If it is a conditioned response, one which can be elicited by such things as positive secondary reinforcers, being loved, a dose of Serutan, manipulations of a chiropractor, or a pink-sugar placebo pill, then we can raise the question, what is the original, or unconditioned, stimulus? I suggest that in the human it is the actual ministrations of a loving mother who cuddles a child as she feeds him and changes his clothes. After all, what is more dramatic evidence of loss of spirit than the anaclitic depressions reported by Spitz, and the cases of marasmus which Ribble made so much of, which all followed withdrawal from tender, loving, maternal care. I am reminded here, too, of the more recent "activist" theories of emotion as propounded by Arnold, Duffy, and Lindsley.

Parenthetically, we have long looked for some means of resolving the dualism between mind, or spirit, and body. I think that we may have found it, when we look at man as an organization of interlocking systems, each observable and describable by appropriate techniques. What has been called mind, soul, or spirit has hitherto been deemed a separate realm of reality, separate and apart from material reality. Suppose, however, we regard the spirit as a mode of organization and the mind as but another system—the perceptual cognitive system. It is affected by other systems, and it affects other systems. It can be studied by appropriate techniques, such as elicitation of disclosure, either spontaneous introspection, or responses to ink-blots. The man's phenomenal field, of which his body image is a part, affects and is affected by the state of the rest of his body system. Its contents are also affected by culturally patterned life experiences. These culturally patterned life experiences also affect the man's body.

What has all this to do with body image? I begin to think that Fisher and Cleveland's work, which shows that it *matters* how a person unconsciously conceptualizes his body, is related to our speculations about spirit. It may well be that a firmly but flexibly bounded body image, as conceived by a person and as projected in responses to ink-blots, is one indicant of optimum spirit-titre.

I suggested earlier that an optimally organized self-structure, accompanied by worth-while goals in life, was a concomitant or condition of optimum bodily defense against entropy, and a condition of optimum behavioral output. I think that the body image, as projected in ink-blots and scored by the methods of Fisher and Cleveland, may well be subtle indicants of a person's present spirit-titre. The body image, with its hypothetical boundaries, doubtless is "built in" as a consequence of socialization experiences. We know that chronic mode of organization of the person-body-milieu system—personality —is an outcome of socialization experiences. Body image and spirit both are likely affected by the design and meaning for life that we call culture.

I think that we may be on the brink of something akin to a conceptual breakthrough, one which is made possible by the explorations in culture, self, body image, general systems theory, and cybernetics. When you get right down to it, a person's experience of his body, of his external physical and social world, and his culture all meet in his phenomenal field and its less conscious substrates. It should not be too much of a surprise to us to learn that there may be relationships among culture, the way the body is conceptualized, and health—relationships which artists through the ages have captured in language that includes terms like soul and spirit.

What research implications follow from all of this? I don't want to sabotage research into body image. Indeed, Secord and I (Jourard and Secord, 1955) made some rather simple demonstrations that feelings about the body are significant personality variables. But I now believe that body image as our chairman conceptualizes it is a happy, but not singular, indicant of more complex states of affairs, including levels of wellness, or personality-health. It may be fruitful to re-examine some old questions in the light of my speculations about spirit, inspiritation, and determiners thereof. Let us look again at suggestibility, "yielding," propaganda, culture, hope, religion, faith, appearance, placebos, and love, and try to discern what effect the central and disclosable and measurable dimensions of these phenomena have for the integrity and wellness of the whole man.

II

Transparency, Spirit, and Healthy Personality*

Let us first acknowledge that positive mental health, or healthy personality, is a concept with different meaning than "normality." By normal personality, I mean those patterns of behavior which are common or typical in a specified group—the kinds of things sociologists tabulate. Stated another way, normal behavior can conveniently be viewed as a class of operant responses which produce the outcome "perceived conformity with social norms" or "perceived non-deviation from norms." From this point of view, normal personality is the sum of all operants and expressive reactions which are reinforced by perceived approval from others or by avoidance of expected punishment from others.

Moral philosophers, ministers, and existentialists tell us, however, that man has more to do with his energies than use them merely to produce popularity, approval, or mediocre anonymity in the mass. Yet many people seek these outcomes to action as ends in themselves, as *summa boni* to which all other considerations are subordinated. The curious thing is that, if a man places normality (as I have defined it) at the pinnacle of importance, many other values are in fact jeopardized. It seems to be a matter of indifference to the social system whether such conformity is achieved by individuals at the price of idiosyncratic need-gratifications, a sense of identity and self-hood, creativity, or even physical health. But such official indifference to all but man's role-conformity has longer-run deleterious effects on the social system. It costs the system progress and innovation. It makes for a "closed" and stagnant society rather than one which is "open" (Popper, 1950).

* Presented at the 1960 meetings of the Southeastern Psychological Association, Atlanta, Georgia.

It is a truth that normality in some social systems is often purchased at the cost of physical illness of gradual onset; and if too many real, idiosyncratic needs are stifled in the pursuit and maintenance of normality, then boredom, neurosis, or psychosis will be regular, predictable outcomes.

The "sociology of illness" tabulates incidences of assorted diseases in various age, sex, socio-economic, and subcultural groupings—incidences which exceed those found in the population at large. For example, peptic ulcer occurs more commonly among men than among women, and schizophrenia occurs more commonly among lower-class people than among upper-middle-class folk. These correlations should not come as any surprise, for the illnesses arise for one reason, and one reason only: *the people who live the ways of life typical to their "ecological niches" become ill because they behave in ways exquisitely calculated to produce just those outcomes.* Stated another way, they become ill because their behavior has been unwittingly selected for its power to achieve role-conformity, not high-level health.

Health is a value concept. Hartman (1958), in his superb paper on axiology, states that anything is good when it fulfills its concept. This philosopher tells us point-blank that *we* must define the concept, "health." Health is not given in nature. If anything is "given," it is chaos, entropy, or random states. Health for humans is a *preferred* mode of organization, one which mediates valued output with minimum jeopardy to the integrity of the outputting system, man. Naturally, we must define this valued output, behavior, for it will vary with age, society, culture, and other factors. But there probably are constant values, within a given range, for the *inputs* necessary to produce and maintain a psychobiological structure which mediates the valued outputs. We have been accustomed to call these inputs "needs," as if the word "need" were somehow self-explanatory. I always wonder, when someone speaks of need, "*What* does a person need, and what does he need it *for?*" Need always has reference to some *outcome* which is valued by somebody. I need food to sustain energy and health. If I don't value energy or health, do I need food? A child is said to need love. What does he need it for? It is a neutral fact that without loving actions on the part of parents, the child will not survive, or if he does, he will not grow in desired ways. It would be more apt to say that parents, who want children to grow in certain directions, *need to love* their children. The child can be said to need love only when he has reached the age where he can pick his goals and diagnose what *he* needs in order to achieve them.

Suppose I define health—mental and physical health —*as an outcome to behavior*, just as normality is an outcome. In principle, there is, or must be, ways for a person to behave, fed by suitable inputs, and guided by appropriate information, which produces, from moment to moment throughout life, an example of structure, function, and behavior which judges would call "healthy"; they like what they see because it is congruent with their explicitly defined concept of health. For the moment, let us postpone the specification of the criteria of health, and focus on behavior.

TRANSPARENCY

It should be true that healthy behavior feels "right" and actually produces both growth and integrity of the system, "man." By integrity I mean resistance to illness, disintegration, or disorganization—all nonvalued or negatively valued states. Doubtless, when a person is behaving in ways that do violence to the integrity of his system, warning signals are emitted. If only man could recognize these, diagnose them himself, and institute corrective action! Then he would live a hundred years. This fact (of warning signals) is capitalized upon by designers of machines; they build indicators which flash lights when output exceeds tolerances or when intakes are outside a specified range. Fuses blow, governors go into action, and power is shut off. "Normal," self-alienated man, however, often ignores his "tilt" signals—anxiety, guilt, fatigue, boredom, pain, or frustration—and continues actions aimed at wealth, power, or normality *until the machine stops.* The meaning of sickness is *protest;* it is the protest of a system which has sent warning signals to the communication center, only to have these ignored. If ignored long enough, the system will no longer mediate even normal behavior, much less optimum behavior. Sickness saves the remnant of the system from total destruction by preventing further operation, until "needs"—inputs— are taken care of. In fact, "being sick"—taking to bed— is itself operant behavior undertaken so as to restore integrity. It is often the only operant behavior a person has available in our culture to secure some kinds of satisfactions which his "normal" mode of action fails to produce, e.g., passivity, "being." As our interest is turning currently to "being," I would like to say that it is only when man *is* sick that society and *he* permit him to *be*, in the presence of others. What a tragedy that, in our society, the only "being" we are permitted by others and which we permit ourselves is being sick, and sometimes being drunk!

The specification of what is needed for physical growth and stamina has been fairly adequately worked out by nutritionists. Maslow (1954), Fromm (1955), Dunn (1959), and others have all tried to specify "psychological" desiderata for optimum mental health. The experience of psychosomatic physicians clearly shows that any physical-psychological dichotomy is ridiculous. For example, food intake may rise or fall beyond optimum limits when a man is in despair over loss of love or identity.

We might say that normal man, who has about ten or so episodes of physical illness a year (Hinkle and Wolff, 1958), pays this price in order to sustain his "normal" way of life, his job, his reputation, his present biased self-concept, and a few other values that are important to him. The measure of importance for any human value is the sheer amount of time and operant behavior devoted to its achievement and defense. Since we spend so much time defending our present self-concepts and our reputation even when this defense fosters self-alienation and costs us our more ultimate health and growth, then these values must be more important than being, wellness, wholeness, growth, and integrity in spite of sanctimonious verbal commitment to the supposedly higher values.

Thus far, I have suggested that people become ill when

they fail to notice and/or act upon the vague discomfort signals which arise when their behavior output and varieties of intake have not been adequate to sustain high-level wellness. (I am omitting discussion of more obvious stresses and privations which exceed modal tolerance as causes of illness.) People are more sensitized to early signals which forecast imminent danger to their jobs, to their automobiles, or other external possessions they value. They develop more dramatic symptoms of neurosis, psychosis, or stress-disease, *as if by surprise*. It is as if they are as opaque to themselves as they strive to be before others. When a car collapses, warning signs were surely available, but likely were neither sought nor noticed. Surely there is research implication here—exploring differences between those who are frequently ill, or seriously ill, and those who sustain more chronic wellness, in the degree of rational interest they display toward their inner experience and the accuracy with which they label inner, vague discomfort, diagnose its causes, and correct these. In this connection, it seems to be true that those people who have "been" and disclosed themselves most fully to another person are most able to acknowledge and diagnose their inner experience. Transparency before another seems to be a condition for transparency to oneself. This is a lesson which more than six decades of psychotherapeutic practice should surely have taught us.

SPIRIT

Now, let us look at another aspect of positive health. Here I have reference to the goals and purposes for which a man uses himself—the meaning of his existence—to attain or fulfill which he utilizes his present psychological and physical structure, whatever its assorted strengths and weaknesses. Halbert Dunn (1959) speaks in this connection of "high-level wellness" and defines it as "an integrated method of functioning which is oriented toward maximizing the potential of which the individual is capable, within the environment where he is functioning. . . ." (It) involves (1) *direction in progress forward and upward* toward a higher potential of functioning, (2) *an open-ended and ever-expanding tomorrow* with its challenge to live at a fuller potential, and (3) *the integration of the whole being of the total individual*—his body, mind, and spirit (goals, purpose, meanings)—in the functioning process (Dunn, 1959b, p. 447).

In another context, Dunn (1959a, p. 788), urges us not to ignore man's spirit, which he says "stems largely from within him. Consequently, we must find ways of making him more aware of his inner world . . ." (Dunn, 1959, p. 788). I take the liberty here of interpreting spirit as "goals or purposes for living," e.g., we speak of "spiritual advisers." I believe we will find that a man who pursues "inspiriting goals" actualizes his potentials and resists illness more effectively than people who have not found, or who have lost, their identity and direction.

Doubtless this complex matter is something experts in research on motivation might learn to measure. Whatever we know about "morale" is probably pertinent in this connection. We need to learn more about hope and will to live—their conditions and their physiological substrate. There is ample reason to suspect that people fall ill, with physical or psychiatric symptoms, because their past way of life not only has failed to "inspirit" (sustain wellness and also happiness), but because the present and future seem to the person to be devoid of hope or meaning or worth-while purpose. Frankl (1959) tells us, in his magnificent book *From Death Camp to Existentialism* that the inmates who could find meaning in their suffering, and who had a purpose for living, survived incredible stress. Medical and nursing lore is bristling with unsystematic accounts of patients who had miraculous recoveries from supposedly terminal illness when someone inspired hope and a purpose for ongoing life. Freud lasted 15 or 20 years with a terrible mouth cancer, perhaps because he had not finished what he had started; he had a mission to complete. We know also that people become well when they have been treated by methods *in which they have faith*. Hence the placebo effect in psychotherapy and medical therapy. Hence faith-healing. Hence the efficacy of Christian Science, chiropractic, medicine men, and other supposedly inexplicable curative agents (Frank, 1961). It appears that man can inspire in man an attitude, goal, or purpose which so affects him (are there measurable brain-events corresponding to hope or spirit?) that his entire psychosomatic unit becomes re-integrated, thereby mediating once more an ongoing output of valued operants which in turn foster further growth and learning and maximize resistance to germs and psychosis.

Doubtless, people become more susceptible to infection when they are hopeless, without direction, or as I call it, dispirited. When life dispirits them, they become ill. Schmale (1958) found, for example, that almost all the patients admitted to a general hospital with organic illness during a one-month period had sustained some emotional crisis involving object-relations shortly before the onset of their physical symptoms. Engel (1958, p. 323) cites evidence strongly suggestive that dispiriting events which induce hopelessness are factors in the onset of ulcerative colitis. We need to look more closely into this. When society does not permit people a way of life that produces rich satisfaction of human needs (in Maslow's (1954) or Fromm's (1955) sense of universal human needs), including the need for meaning in the present and in the future, then gradually dispiritation begins, and physical or mental illness takes root. There is much about normality, or respectability, which leads inexorably to stress, lowered resistance, sapped ego strength, and physical or mental illness. This means that if we treasure health, we have got to redefine the values by which men live—permit people to be themselves, to satisfy more needs and to acknowledge more self than seems presently to be the case. We even have to inculcate the value of being oneself, over and above our role-responsibilities. We have, in short, to re-define normality. Existentialists are trying to do this, and they may succeed. They are trying to discover content for the present void in the official, scientifically based concept of the *subjective* side of man.

To state the above considerations in terms of the individual, we can say that a man will remain most energetic, most resistant to illness, most creative, when social mores and socialization permit him to acknowledge without shame a broader range of his real self; when goals, meanings and purposes are available which challenge man to use his creativity and his energy; when man learns from Kierkegaard that despair means not being oneself.

Nothing makes a man sick sooner than feeling useless, unwanted, unchallenged, and unneeded, or the feeling that the values other men pursue are empty and joyless for him. This is what happens to many men who retire from work at 65, and they die soon thereafter.

What research implications have we here? We can seek to discover indices of motivation or commitment to life. We can explore the stimulus or environmental conditions for the subjective response, "Life is worth living." We can discover methods for assessing a man's present hierarchy of values—the ones to which he actually devotes his operant behavior—in order to discern whether his behavior sustains wellness as well as it produces riches, fame, or popularity. We can seek to identify the vast population of people who are secretly bored or unhappy and compare them on pertinent dimensions with men with a mission and a purpose which sustains them, like Schweitzer, Freud, Russell, Chaplin, and other ageless people, into long productive lives. Some pertinent dimensions are self-disclosure, the nature of the goals to which they commit their energies, how they play, how much they are themselves in interpersonal transactions, and their degree of empathy and knowledge of others.

HEALTHY PERSONALITY

Thus far, I have pointed to two researchable factors in healthy personality—degree of cognizance of inner experience and the relationship between subjective states of meaning, hope, or purpose and mental and physical health. Incidentally, I recommend looking at Fisher and Cleveland's (1958) work on body-image boundaries in this connection. Now, I would like briefly to turn to the question of defining healthy personality—the observable symptoms which in the opinion of competent judges betoken positive mental health. It is clear that this is a matter of values, of consensual definition during any given epoch. However, there appears to be a considerable degree of consensus now in existence. I found it possible to outline some of the characteristics of healthy personality in my book *Personal Adjustment* (Jourard, 1958).

I attempted to define healthy instrumental behavior, healthy emotional behavior, healthy sexual behavior, healthy cognitive behavior, healthy interpersonal behavior, a healthy self-structure, a healthy conscience, healthy transactions between a person and his body, and some objective features of loving behavior. Jahoda (1958) presented a more systematic, research-oriented summary of essentially the same literature I consulted. I believe that these works show that we are in a position in which we could, if some agency were willing to underwrite the cost, actually produce a scale for measuring levels of total health, ranging from moribundity to the epitome of wellness. Given such a quantitative yardstick, it would become a routine matter then to identify the independent variables of which health scores were functions. For my own amusement, I once constructed just such a yardstick, and though it wants validation, for example, by the method of critical incidents or by some of the better-known psychometric standardization procedures, yet I found that I could reliably rate people whom I knew, who varied from severe physical and mental illness at one extreme to high-level living at the other.

If I might be permitted to prophesy, I think that when we learn how to measure the pertinent variables we are going to find a factor which highly loads such variables as: the values and purposes which a man affirms and pursues; degree of integration of the components of the self-structure; creativity and inspiration; optimal resistance to physical illness; profound contact with inner reality; a high degree of empathy with others; ability to eat, sleep, and excrete well; ability to work, play, and love with gusto; absence of psychosis; ability to be and to disclose oneself when with others. In thinking about health, I like to conjure up the image of a family of germs looking for a home in which they might multiply and flourish. If I were the leader of such a family of germs and had the well-being of my family at heart, I would avoid any man like the plague so long as he was productively and enjoyably engaged in living and loving. I would wait until he lost hope, or became discouraged, or became ground down by the requirements of respect-

able role-playing. At that precise moment, I would in-
vade; his body would then become as fertile a life-space
for my breed of germs as a well-manured flower-bed is for
the geranium or the weed.

Part V

A New Way of Being for Nurses

12

Away with the "Bedside Manner"! *

Many nurses acquire a fixed way of behaving in the presence of patients which might best be called their bedside manner. Some nurses always smile, others hum, and still others answer all patients' questions about medication with the automatic phrase, "This will make you feel better." The bedside manner appears to be something which the nurse "puts on" when she dons her uniform.

As an observer in a hospital situation, I recently noticed some instances of the bedside manner which led me to wonder about the function of this particular pattern of interpersonal behavior. For example, I was in a patient's room, interviewing him informally about his background and current preoccupations, and on several occasions nurses entered the room to perform various "nursing functions." This man was seriously ill and had much on his mind, but his nurses came in talking cheerfully and did not cease the cheerful discourse until they had left. I had little doubt that the nurses knew no more about this man after they left than they knew when they entered. I verified this guess when I later asked the nurses to tell me about Mr. Jones. One nurse replied, "Oh, he's a nice fellow." The other told me, "He's O.K., though sometimes he's a bit difficult." I asked both of them if they had any idea of what Mr. Jones had on his mind, and each said that *so far as she knew*, he was cheerful most of the time.

It became apparent that these nurses, who after all are not atypical, had "solved the human relations problem" in nursing by means of stereotyped modes of behavior. Now I would like to discuss the bedside manner in the light of more recent formulations of interpersonal behavior—its origins, functions, and connections with nursing care.

* Presented January 9, 1959, at a meeting of the Faculty Training Group, University of Florida, College of Nursing.

Interpersonal behavior is any and all behavior which a person undertakes in the presence of others. From a sociological point of view, patterned interpersonal behavior is described as role-performance, and it serves an important function in the social system (the hospital, for example) to accomplish the purposes for which it was organized.

From a psychological point of view, interpersonal behavior patterns are acquired as means for satisfying needs and for reducing anxiety. *Rigid* interpersonal behavior has been called "character armor" by some psychoanalysts (Reich, 1948). It serves the function of stifling spontaneity in the person and protecting the person from possible hurt coming from the outside. Character armor serves effectively to hide a person's real self, both from himself and from others. Character armor is acquired in situations marked by anxiety, and it protects a person from recurrences of anxiety—and from guilt-provoking impulses and actions.

Doubtless, the "bedside manner" warrants being regarded as an instance of character armor, since it is a case of rigid interpersonal behavior. It is acquired by a nurse as a means of coping with the anxieties engendered by repeated encounters with suffering, demanding patients. If her "armor" is effective, it permits the nurse to go about her duties unaffected by any disturbing feelings of pity, anger, inadequacy, or insecurity. It is as if the nurse, early in training, asked herself the question, "How should I behave in the presence of patients?" By trial and error, or perhaps through emulation of a highly esteemed instructor, she arrives at a "formula" which "works" for her. Hence, one nurse might habitually crack jokes, another might look and act hurried, and still another might "mother" all her patients on the premise that all patients are babies.

But let us look more closely at these stereotyped interpersonal behavior patterns to see some consequences to which they lead. We know that one person's behavior toward another is a controlling factor in the behavior of the other person. Thus, maternal behavior tends to "pull" dependent behavior from the other person (Leary, 1957). Joking behavior tends to evoke joking behavior in return from the other. Careful analysis of psychotherapy patients has shown that not only they, but people in general, are able to function most comfortably with other people when the *latter limit their reactions to some fixed range*. Some people are unable to cope with another's tears, some cannot handle another's anger, some cannot deal with another's sexuality, and still others cannot tolerate spontaneous expressions of despair. Unwittingly, they behave in the presence of others so that the others will find it difficult to express these threatening patterns of behavior. We may assume, then, that *one of the latent functions of the bedside manner is to reduce the probability that patients will behave in ways that are likely to threaten the nurse.*

There is, however, a consequence of rigid interpersonal behavior, such as is exemplified by the bedside manner, which can gravely interfere with the avowed aims of the nursing profession. The nursing profession is dedicated to the promotion of health and well-being in patients, to co-operation with the forces that abet recovery from illness. Nurses traditionally pursue these professional aims through such means as administering medications, providing physical care, and ensuring that standards of hygiene and physical comfort are maintained so long as the patient is in their care. No self-respecting nurse would overlook such vital information as the patient's temperature, blood-pressure, and other physical signs of progress or regress with respect to recovery. *Yet, the bedside manner is nicely designed to exclude a highly important source of information that has much pertinence to the optimum response of the patient to treatment. I have reference here to information which can only be obtained through the patient's verbal disclosure of what is on his mind.* Just as thermometers and sphygmomanometers reveal something about the state of the patient's body—which nurses and physicians are concerned with—so does verbal self-disclosure reveal something about the state of the patient as a whole person. If the patient has something on his mind, it is possible, even likely, that this "something" may have direct pertinence to his over-all problem in health. Thus, he may be gravely worried, or he may have serious misconceptions about his illness, or

he may know that he is markedly sensitive to penicillin.
I know of several instances of people who nearly died because every time they tried to tell their nurse of their
intolerance of penicillin the nurse replied, cheerfully and
firmly, as she neatly performed the injection, "The doctor
knows what's best; this will help you get well." Nobody
listened. We may propose, then, that *another latent function of the bedside manner is to prevent a patient from
disclosing himself, to prevent patients from making themselves known to their nurses (and physicians)*. Rigid interpersonal behavior presumes that all people before
whom it is enacted are alike in personality; to some extent, rigid interpersonal behavior actually provokes a
certain uniformity in the behavior of others. But we know
that, in spite of certain fundamental human similarities
between people, they differ markedly one from the other.
It is apparent, then, that *the bedside manner seeks to
obliterate or to deny individuality in patients;* it unconsciously attempts to enforce a certain uniformity in
patients' personalities, the kind of uniformity with which
the nurse feels most competent to cope. It seems to be
difficult for nurses (and others) to accept the fact that
they cannot know any other person—patient, student,
friend, or family member—*until they have taken steps to
find out who and how he is*. Recently, professional nurses
and nursing educators have become concerned with
attempts to "integrate psychiatric and mental health concepts into nursing curricula and programs of nursing care."
Translation of this weighty and worth-while assignment
into achievable aims is problematic. It is well to ask,
"What psychiatric and mental health concepts? How
does one go about 'integrating' (or as one participant in
a recent conference proposed, in all seriousness, 'homog-
enizing') these concepts into a curriculum and a nurs-
ing-care program?"

We have proposed that one important concept, or
precept, stemming from the experience of psychiatrists
and mental-hygiene workers is as follows: "It is important
to know the other person's 'self,' that is, how he is experiencing the world. It is important to know the other
person's self because his behavior, and even his physiology,
is affected by his 'phenomenal field.' Workers, such as

nurses and physicians, who are committed to changing physiology from the pathological range to the healthy range are obliged to learn as much information about a given person as is pertinent to their aims. If they overlook information available only through patients' full disclosure of self, then they are, in a sense, possibly hamstringing their diagnostic and therapeutic endeavors.

"Let it be granted, then, that knowledge about a patient's 'self' is of value for medical and nursing care. But we have already shown that a stereotyped pattern of interpersonal behavior enacted by many nurses—the bedside manner—is nicely designed to prevent patients from disclosing themselves. It becomes apparent, then, that *the bedside manner can actually obstruct* (or at the very least not help) *attempts to "integrate psychiatric and mental health concepts into programs of nursing education and nursing care."*

Another concept, or principle, which stems from the broad field of mental health maintains that "real-self being" is an aspect of healthy personality. Neurotic people, and people with the "socially patterned defects" whom Fromm (1955) and Horney (1950) described so aptly, are all persons who display varying degrees of "self-alienation." Concretely, this means that they have repressed or suppressed much of their own real and spontaneous reactions to experience. They replace their spontaneous behavior with carefully censored behavior which conforms to a rigid role-definition, or a rigid and highly limited self-concept. They behave as they "should" behave and feel what they "should" feel. When roles and/or self-concepts exclude too much "real self," a person soon experiences certain symptoms, viz., vague anxiety, depression, and boredom, and if the person has come to neglect the needs and feelings of his body, then such physical symptoms as unwarranted fatigue, headache, and digestive upsets will arise. In short, failure or inability to know and be one's real self can make one sick. In extreme cases, where the real self has been well-nigh strangulated, it may happen that there is a "breakthrough," and the person suffers a "nervous breakdown."

People squelch their real selves because they have learned to fear the consequences of real-self being. I have observed that the nurses' bedside manner is not a faithful portrayal of her real self. Is it possible that the role of nurse, as this has been learned during training and in practice, is one which is detrimental to the physical and mental health of nurses? Is it possible that nurses, in their attempts to root out their own spontaneity, replacing it with stereotyped modes of interpersonal behavior, are actually doing violence to their own personalities and bodies? We may propose that *another latent function of the bedside manner is to foster increasing self-alienation in nurses, thus jeopardizing their own health and well-being.*

There is a connection between a nurse's inability or fear to be her real self while "on duty" and the blocking of patients' self-disclosure. Research and clinical practice show that one of the factors which promotes real-self being and honest self-disclosure in a person is an empathic acknowledgment of what has been expressed. Now, if a nurse is afraid and even ignorant of her own self, she is highly likely to be threatened by a patients' real-self expressions. Hence, a patient might send out a "trial balloon" concerning what really is on his mind, only to be encountered with a response from the nurse which effectively squelches him. A nurse who is more aware of the breadth and depth of her own real self is in a much better position to "empathize" with her patients and to encourage (or at least not block) their self-disclosure. The bedside manner, then, can blind a nurse to much of her own real self; the consequent reduction in insight then impairs empathy with patients. Empathy—the ability to guess what a patient is experiencing in a given situation—is an outgrowth of insight, or self-awareness. *The bedside manner desensitizes a nurse to her own experience and handicaps her attempts to know her patient.*

We have pointed out that the bedside manner was originally acquired as a kind of protection for the nurse: it kept her relations with patients impersonal and protected her both against becoming known by patients and also against any feelings she might have for patients which she believes she should not have. Suppose one could "strip" a nurse of her bedside manner, just as one could divest her of her uniform? If a person is proud of his or her body's appearance, nakedness will not be much of a threat. If a person is not ashamed of his real self, then disclosure of self should not be highly threatening either. But here is a paradox noticeable in the training of nurses. Beginning students, both in colleges of nursing and in hospital schools of nursing, begin their careers loaded with responsiveness—real-self responsiveness—to the experiences which confront them. They experience and sometimes express feelings of panic, disgust at excreta, shame at exposures of the human body—the gamut of reactions which one might expect from naïve late adolescents. They compare their own feelings and reactions with the examples provided them by their teachers and preceptors and find themselves "inferior." They may even be directly told, "Nurses don't feel like that." Now, in time many of the initial emotional reactions undergone by beginning students will change. The initial shyness in the presence of another's nakedness may change to frank acceptance of nudity. As the girl matures and has more experience with a broader range of human reactions (her own and those of others), her emotional responses to giving injections or enemas may change radically from what they were early in training. But this "real-self" change will not occur unless the student nurse has been able to acknowledge and express her feelings openly and test all of her expectations with regard to the provoking experiences. If the student has been obliged to deny to her instructors and to herself that she has certain feelings, then she may eventually become ashamed and afraid of her real self. Consequently, she suppresses and represses her honest reactions and replaces them insofar as she is able with what she believes she "should" feel. In time, following the role-models available to her, she becomes a nurse with a squelched real-self and a contrived bedside manner. It seems likely that the bedside manner which we have been commenting upon is a direct outgrowth of the instructional period in school or college and the apprenticeship period when the student is watching how experienced nurses carry out their work. Stated another way, it seems very likely that students actively learn and are actively taught to be estranged from their real selves —more estranged than their family roles required them to be—and so it is no accident that they arrive at graduation with a cool (or contrived warm) bedside manner.

What alternative is available for nurses to take the place of a bedside manner which seems to defeat many of the aims of the nursing profession? How can nurses with a confirmed bedside manner get rid of it, and how can students be trained so that they will not have chronic need to hide their real selves behind a professional mask? Observation has shown that experienced nurses who have been fortunate enough, following a "nervous breakdown," to undergo intensive psychotherapy, will abandon their prior rigid interpersonal patterns with patients, displaying greater insight into themselves and greater empathy with their patients. They feel and act more freely with their patients and elicit more self-disclosure from patients. This would imply that all nurses should undergo intensive psychotherapy. In fact, this is impracticable, and it is not certain that it would accomplish its aim. There is growing evidence to show, however, that the average nurse can increase her ability both to promote self-disclosure in patients and to utilize the disclosures as guides for more personalized, "tailor-made" nursing actions. The most direct and simple step which she can take in this direction is to make use of all available time, whether it be 10 seconds or half an hour, to permit the patient to talk about what is on his mind. This does not mean formal interviewing. Rather, it implies simply taking steps to become acquainted with this very person to whom one is giving an injection or backrub. It will come as a surprise to many nurses when they discover the extent to which they have actually avoided many opportunities to listen to a patient who was bursting to reveal what was on his mind.

The question of training nurses in the direction of greater real-self being is another matter altogether. It seems to call for a radical alteration in their instructor's conception of what nursing education entails. Much learning about what it means to be a nurse occurs informally when students identify with the attitudes and practices displayed by her teachers. If these teachers are impersonal and have an air of perfection and imperturbability about them, the students are likely to pursue this impossible pinnacle of human performance. If the teacher has a "classroom manner" similar to her bedside manner, then it is difficult to see how the student can ever come to care about her own real self, much less the real self of her patients. One evaluates his real self in the manner that significant others evaluate it. If one's teachers are impersonal in their transactions to students, likely the students will be impersonal in their attitude toward themselves. If one's teachers no longer practice active personalized nursing care, but only preach about it, the students likely acquire the concept that teaching's the thing and nursing care is for flunkies. As the teachers are, so will the students become, with the exception of those rebellious students who become their teachers in reverse.

We are beginning to discover that basically normal people can become sensitized and more alert to their own real selves, as well as the real-self expressions of others, without recourse to intensive psychotherapy or technical books on psychodynamics. In fact, the two kinds of alertness seem to grow together. Possibly then, if all nurses who are in an instructional role become less afraid to disclose themselves to their students and proceed to do so, the students will acquire more realistic and feasible role-models with which to identify. If teachers will show a greater interest in knowing the real selves of the students whom they teach, they will doubtless foster greater acknowledgment of their real selves by the students. An interest in and an acknowledgment of the full gamut of inner experience in oneself and in others is contagious—just as contagious as is impersonality and indifference to inner experience. It may be proposed as a testable hypothesis that if nursing faculty in colleges and schools become more capable of acknowledging their own inner experience apropos their subject matter and patient contacts, disclosing this to students; and if the faculty acknowledge the feelings of their students, granting them the freedom to have all kinds of feelings; and if the faculty actually practice both nursing and teaching of students on the basis of this greater insight and empathy —then students will learn (or not unlearn) how to be themselves with patients. Doubtless, a regime of this sort would abolish the contrived, tense, even frantic, and sometimes silly specimen of behavior that we have called the bedside manner.

13

Getting Mental Health Into Nursing*

Educators in the health professions have sought to "integrate concepts" from the disciplines of psychology, sociology, anthropology, and psychiatry into their basic curricula, presumably with a view toward improving the quality of professional practice. Doubtless, this concern is an outgrowth of discontent on the part of professional person and client alike with the often impersonal nature of professional care. In medicine and nursing, toward which professions this chapter is primarily directed, there is a further reason for concern with "integration." I have reference here to the increasing conviction, based on experience of psychiatrists, that a patient's "self" and the nature of the physician-patient and nurse-patient *relationship* are factors in the patient's illness and recovery.

When we look afresh at the unwieldy jargon of the "integration" assignment (professional educators seem to be no different from other disciplines in their predilection for untranslatable technical terms), we are impelled to inquire, "What is a mental health concept? A psychiatric concept? How does one go about 'integrating' these things? How can anyone tell when 'integration' has been accomplished?" As a matter of fact, I once paralyzed for several minutes the proceedings of a conference in nursing that was devoted to discussion of ways and means of "integrating" merely by raising those questions. Happily enough, the questions were tabled, and the conference got down to its proper business of discussion.

In my work at a nursing college, I addressed myself to the questions inherent in the problem of "integrating mental health and psychiatric concepts," and I have

* Prepared February 2, 1959, for the Faculty Training Group, University of Florida, College of Nursing, and published in the *Canadian Nurse Journal*, April, 1962.

arrived at a direction of thinking which seems to hold
some promise of answering these questions in a workable
and feasible way. I sought to look at the professional-
person-client relationship from a viewpoint sufficiently
detached to enable me to identify pertinent variables in
the helping transaction, and then I tried to determine
just what it was that the educators wanted from "mental
health" disciplines—mainly psychiatry and psychology.
Furthermore, I tried to ascertain what these disciplines
actually had to offer. The present paper is an attempt to
outline a working conception of what mental health
disciplines have to offer medicine and nursing, together
with some suggestions regarding the manner and mani-
festations of their "integration."

Let us first look at man. He can readily be "dissected,"
both conceptually and literally, into a number of component systems, e.g., his circulatory system, endocrine
system, nervous system, excretory system, etc. Students of
these "systems"—specialists—provide the beginning or
the general practitioner with knowledge of the range
within which the repective organs and functions vary in
wellness and disease. The practitioner is then able, with
a given patient, to observe and measure these systems,
employing the observations for the diagnosis of illness
and as criteria for progress in treatment. The nonspecial-
izing practitioner doesn't know all there is to know about
each system, but he doesn't have to; he does, however,
know that his job calls for him to be acquainted with
some knowledge of these systems, and he conscientiously
observes them when he is making routine observations
on any patient. Routinely, most physicians will check a
patient's pulse and temperature, because it has been
learned that the behavior of the heart and the body-
temperature are sensitive indices of the degree of wellness of the entire body. Such routine attention to these
phenomena doubtless illustrates the successful "integration of physiological concepts into medical education and
practice."

Psychological science has addressed itself to systematic
study of man's inner experience and his overt behavior.
These comprise his dependent variables, and he investi-
gates their dependence upon myriads of pertinent inde-

pendent variables. Behavioristic psychologists limit themselves primarily to the analysis of the *stimulus* control of behavior, but their findings have had little to offer a clinical practitioner. The "phenomenological" psychologists—those concerned with man's subjective side, i.e., with his "self," his inner experience—have convincingly shown that man responds, not to stimuli *per se*, but rather to the *meanings* which stimuli have for him. These psychologists have introduced the concept of the *phenomenal field* to describe the sum total of a man's conscious experience at any given moment (Combs and Snygg, 1959). The phenomenal field includes an individual's perceptions, beliefs, imaginings, and memories, and it also includes a system of cognitions called the *self-structure* (Jourard, 1958, pp. 241-242). This latter term refers to the beliefs, feelings, and ideals which an individual holds with regard to his own personality. I would like to propose that this complex perceptual-cognitive system—the phenomenal field—is the *variable* which, when "integrated" into medical and nursing curricula and practice, will bring about the outcomes which educators have sought, viz., more personalized care of patients, more apt diagnoses, and more effective therapy. While much of what follows seems banal and obvious, yet I am convinced that the explicit statement of the "obvious" has value, if for no other reason than to permit critical assessment. Furthermore, the manner in which the exposition develops throws light on the ways in which "integration" might be accomplished.

We have asserted that man's phenomenal field is a crucial variable in man's behavior. This clearly implies that if we would understand man's overt behavior, *we must become acquainted with the contents of his phenomenal field*. We are obliged to learn what he is thinking and feeling and what the things in the world mean to him. It is also pertinent to assert that *man's phenomenal field affects and is affected by the functioning of the various anatomical and physiological systems*. Circulation, respiration, blood-chemistry, and other systems are known to vary with the emotional state of man.

Thus, if a man's behavior and over-all physical condition are to be fully understood, we must pay due attention to his phenomenal field. This raises the question, "How does one get to know a person's phenomenal field?" If we regard the phenomenal field as a species of gauge, or recording instrument, we can ask, "How does a practitioner make the readings?"

It is possible to guess at a man's probable inner experience—this is what empathy entails—but guessing is rather unreliable. A more direct, perhaps the most direct, means of obtaining "readings" from a man's phenomenal field is to encourage and permit the man to disclose in words and gestures just what he is experiencing, what he sees, feels, believes, and remembers. A person's *self-disclosures* constitute the equivalent of the numbers on a thermometer; the disclosures are the person's attempt to communicate to the doctor or nurse just how the world and his body seem to him. There is reason to suspect that the phenomenal field is an even more sensitive indicator or gauge of the over-all condition of a person than, say, the pulse rate. Now, anyone who can count can take a pulse reading. Anyone who can hear can take a phenomenal-field "reading." But all data, whether tracings from an EKG, numbers from a manometer, or the self-disclosures of a patient, call for recording and interpretation before they can be employed helpfully in diagnosis and assessment of progress in therapeutic treatment. Consequently, data of all kinds are kept on records. Anyone who can write can make entries in a medical record; but it takes training and sophistication to be able to "make sense" of the entries that have been made.

With respect to employing phenomenal-field "readings" in medical and nursing practice, two problems arise: (a) How to encourage and permit a patient to disclose his inner experience fully, spontaneously, and truthfully, and (b) How to interpret what has been disclosed. In response to these problems, it may be said that scientific students of interpersonal behavior and man's self-structure have some pertinent answers. Broadly speaking, a person will disclose himself to an interested audience who is warm, permissive, and concerned. Skill in eliciting and reinforcing self-disclosure can be learned, and it is already being taught in college courses in interviewing technique. (Witness the increasing widespread use of the "reflection" technique.) Skill in *interpreting the meaning* (manifest and latent) of disclosures, both verbal and non-verbal, can be learned, but it calls for extensive ground-ing in various basic disciplines, e.g., sociology, psycho-analysis, and personality theory.

But let us look briefly at self-disclosure. Every person has the capacity to disclose the contents of his phe-nomenal field on request, unless these contents conflict with his self-concept, his public self, or his conscience. Under the latter conditions, disclosure may be highly threatening, and the person may refuse to disclose him-self openly, honestly, and spontaneously. In most general terms, we may say that *anxiety* makes a person reluctant to disclose the contents of his phenomenal field to some-one else. This implies that a professional person, such as a nurse, teacher, physician, or psychotherapist, must learn ways of recognizing and coping with the anxieties that inhibit self-disclosure. However, in our culture, people withhold self-disclosure for another, more obvious reason; they believe (often erroneously) that no one is interested in *their* unique view of the world, their thoughts and feelings. Consequently they keep this information to themselves, disclosing only banalities and clichés. If a nurse or teacher conveys a sincere interest in learning what is on the mind of the patient or student, then this reason for avoiding fuller disclosure can easily be by-passed.

It is the thesis of the present paper that "mental health and psychiatric concepts" will have been integrated into health professions' curricula and practice when "readings" from the psychological "gauge"—self-disclosures from the patient—are as routinely obtained, recorded, evaluated, and acted upon as are readings of temperature or blood-pressure, or observations of the dressings and the condi-tion of the room. We have already suggested that the routine interest of the physician in determining pulse, blood-count, urine content, and so forth indicates the "integration of *physiological* concepts into medical cur-ricula and medical practice." Observations of the pulse, the blood, or the urine are made because it is known that these factors vary with the over-all condition of the body; hence such observations facilitate diagnosis and treat-

ment. Now, if there is one single concept or contribution
which psychological science has made to applied fields
such as medicine, nursing, and education, it is this, and
it bears reiteration: Man's phenomenal field, including
his self-structure, is a variable related both to behavior
and to physiology. The content of a man's phenomenal
field is a sensitive indicator of his total organismic state
—either well or ill—just as is the pulse, skin temperature,
or blood chemistry. It may be accepted as a truism that
the phenomenal field is a variable of crucial significance
to medicine, nursing, and all other arts in which one
person is striving to promote change of some sort in another. *When the phenomenal field is not "checked"
routinely in nursing or medicine, a crime of omission is
committed, the gravity of which is no less serious than
failure to make routine physiological checks.* A patient's
phenomenal field constitutes information that may be
highly crucial in arriving at a diagnosis or in planning
therapy. This information is not only pertinent at the
time when a "history" is being taken; the phenomenal
field goes on registering thoughts, feelings, fantasies,
memories, and perceptions, even when a patient is asleep.
In this regard, it is little different from the heart, which
continues to beat 24 hours daily and which is routinely
checked every time a physician encounters a patient.
When a professional person of any sort is face to face
with his client, he is maximally helpful when he refreshes
his concept of the client's condition. This means making all observations that will be pertinent. There is little
basis for assuming that the patient is exactly the same
from hour to hour, and so fresh observations are called
for with every contact. This means that self-disclosure
should be obtained—the phenomenal field should be
checked—every time that a professional person is face
to face with his client. The information obtained from
a patient's disclosures can then be evaluated in its own
right or correlated with other data that are available,
e.g., physiological measures of one kind or another. Thus,
in response to the question "How do you feel?," a patient may say, "I feel just fine," but one may then find
his pulse racing, his blood-pressure high, etc. Discrep-
ancies of this sort (not unlike a primitive lie detector)

will mean something to the physician or nurse responsible for the patient's well-being.

We have mentioned several times that obtaining self-disclosure from a patient is a direct analogy to obtaining data about a patient's blood-pressure; the phenomenal field and the sphygmomanometer are both "gauges" which register data of importance to the practitioner. But there is one crucial difference between the processes of obtaining a blood-pressure reading and a phenomenal-self "reading" that must be noted.

Few patients report an increase in well-being following a blood-pressure reading. Many patients, however, will experience a reduction in anxiety and physical tension, and an increase in feeling of their own identity and worth, following the experience of full self-disclosure to an interested nurse or physician. As Freud early noted, the technique of observation and the mechanism of helping are well-nigh identical in psychotherapy in particular and in interpersonal transactions in general.

What does one do with "readings from the psychological gauge"—a patient's self-disclosure? For that matter, what does a nurse or physician do with blood-pressure and pulse readings? These data are recorded on special charts, they are plotted, and more important, they are used as the basis for evaluating the over-all condition of the patient and his progress in therapy, and as guides to further therapeutic measures. I would guess that, up to the present, self-disclosure data has not been as systematically sought, recorded, charted, and evaluated from day to day as have temperature or blood pressure, nor has it been as systematically employed as a means of assessing progress in therapy or as a guide to therapeutic measures—except perhaps accidentally.

Suppose I were a physician, glancing over a chart that was kept on a patient. Under the heading "Temperature," I would note the daily fluctuations. Under the heading "Bowel Movements," I might notice that these had been carefully charted and evaluated. Under the heading "Patient's *Self*" I might notice *nothing*. This would mean something to me. Or I might notice six brief entries made today for Mr. Jones, who is awaiting an operation for cancer of the rectum:

6:30 a.m.—Mr. Jones said that he feels fine (during breakfast).

9:00 a.m.—As he was receiving an injection, he said "I feel fine."

12:00 noon—Patient reports that he feels just fine.

7:00 p.m.—He says that he feels fine.

9:00 p.m.—He says that he feels fine.

I might look at what has been entered and wonder why he says he feels fine. I don't know what conclusion I might come to, but noting this data would impel me to make further observations.

It could be that the entries (or lack of entries) for "Patient's Self" might reflect nothing more than the fact that no one has systematically shown an interest in making these "readings"; or the trivial nature of the entries may show (to a skilled person) the presence of profound anxiety that has not been medically acknowledged and coped with. Or, the lack of entries may betoken grave neglect of important observations on the part of attending personnel.

Which leads me to an observation about relationships between professional people. Just as a patient may fear to disclose himself to nurse or physician, so might the nurse dread disclosing or reporting—in person or on paper—what she has observed, felt, guessed, and thought in connection with the patient. She may fear being criticized or laughed at. If such is the case, it could well happen that much possibly invaluable information is lost to the physician because he has not heard or read about these observations and hunches. Just as a patient must disclose his "real self" to his doctors and nurses so that they can be maximally helpful in diagnosis and treatment, *so must all who attend the patient disclose the pertinent aspects of their experience with the patient to responsible parties.* Just as a patient's phenomenal field is a most important instrument for recording and reporting what goes on in his whole life-situation, *so is the phenomenal field of the nurse a recording and reporting instrument—often a most sensitive one.* If it is not heard or read by a head nurse or physician, then it is analogous with failure to examine X-rays that have already been made—a loss of possibly important data. Thus, *any fac-*

tor which inhibits disclosure of self on the part of one professional person to another is detrimental to the overall program of diagnosis and therapy for the patient.

Let it be taken as proven with face validity that observations of a patient's phenomenal field, secured by focused interview or through the promotion of self-disclosure while other aspects of care are carried on, is a necessary condition for optimum care, and evidence of the extent of integration of mental-health and psychiatric concepts into general nursing and medical care. It is pertinent to ask, now, "What factors militate against obtaining self-disclosure from patients?"

Perhaps the most general answers to this question are (a) failure of professional people to recognize the importance of phenomenal-field data in an over-all program of diagnosis and treatment, and (b) a dread of "becoming too involved" with patients when the latter are permitted to disclose themselves to a full extent. This dread of becoming overly involved has two justifications that doctors and nurses often mention. One is that "there is too much work to be done, and so time cannot be wasted just talking or listening to patients." The other, possibly deeper reason for blocking self-disclosure in patients is fear of the feelings which patients' disclosures can evoke in the professional person. I would like to comment briefly on the phobia against involvement with patients.

Doctors and nurses often acquire, at some time during their training, the view that to "be professional" means to be without feeling in the face of human misery. Granted, it is of the utmost importance that a physician or nurse not explode into helpless tears or impotent rage when operations are to be performed or difficult diagnoses obtained. But this is not to say that they must be impersonal machines without affect and without the capacity to be affected by the needs and feelings of patients. I have suspected that the "bedside manner," with its false jollity, or assumed omniscience, omnipotence, and imperturbability, are special cases of what psychoanalysts call "character armor" (Reich, 1948) or a "magic cloak" (Moloney, 1949), donned by nurses and physicians to squelch their own feelings and to squelch real-self disclosure in patients. There is ample reason to as-

sume that competent professional work can be done by
people who retain access to their real feelings. *There is
ample reason to suspect that the bedside manner, far
from facilitating competent medical and nursing care,
actually hamstrings such care by producing an unproduc-
tive relationship between the professional person and the
patient.* A patient who feels assured by his doctors' and
nurses' omniscience in the acute stages of his illness may
almost vomit later on, when the professional person enters the sick-room, saying "Well, how are *we* feeling this
morning? Did you take your pink medicine this morning?
Now, don't ask any questions, doctor knows best."
Granted, this is a caricature, but transactions similar to
the caricature have been known to occur in the past.

With respect to failure to recognize the importance of
phenomenal-field data for ongoing diagnosis and therapy,
it may be said that professional schools may produce
such failure by important omissions in their curricula. If
the curricular job had been done well, practicing nurses
or physicians would *feel guilty* if they did not notice and
record pertinent aspects of patients' disclosures, just as
they might now feel guilty of oversight if they failed to
record pulse, blood pressure, laboratory reports, etc.

The foregoing considerations provide us with a convenient and valid basis for assessing the extent to which
any health-profession education program has effectively
integrated mental-health and psychiatric concepts into
its curriculum. One can look for the following sorts of
evidence:

1. To what extent does the professional person strive
to learn each patient's "self" or his phenomenal field?

2. How effective is the given professional person in
promoting full and pertinent disclosure of self in patients?

3. How sophisticated is the professional person in interpreting or evaluating a patient's disclosure (or lack
thereof) as bases for helpful actions or as occasions for
seeking consultative help with a patient?

4. What allowance is made for disclosure data in
charts which are kept on patients at present for other
kinds of information? What is the nature of the entries
which are made concerning patient-disclosures, if any?

5. How alert is the professional person to evidence of anxiety in patients which is not so obvious from the verbatim transcript of his conversation?

6. How able are doctors, nurses, and other health-profession personnel in behaving at a "real-self" level with each other and with patients and in avoiding the grotesque phoniness of the bedside manner?

7. How competent are personnel in establishing personal contact and maintaining contact with the reality of the selves of patients who come from a diversity of age ranges and cultural backgrounds, who suffer a variety of physical ills, and who represent diverse personality structures?

Direct acknowledgment of the importance of patients' phenomenal fields as a factor in their illness and recovery forcefully directs the attention of educators to aspects of their curriculum which enhance or inhibit students' ability to obtain and cope helpfully with self-disclosure in patients. "Interpersonal skill" or "interpersonal competence" then acquires more explicit meaning; in this context, it implies ability to facilitate disclosure in patients, to acknowledge and interpret what has been disclosed, and to use the information as the basis for more accurately "aimed" professional action. Such action may run the gamut from brief psychotherapy, to a factual lecture, to frank admission of inability to cope with the facts that have been learned. On those occasions, the professional person may then call for help from suitable specialists.

Acknowledgment of the importance of patients' phenomenal fields does not necessarily imply that all nurses, physicians, or aides must be fully trained psychotherapists. Psychotherapy is a specialty which seeks to change personality in basic ways, and it calls for special training. However, every practitioner can be trained to recognize the importance of observing patients' inner experience, and every practitioner can be helped to improve in skill at eliciting the necessary self-disclosure. It will be enough for the improvement of over-all medical care if all personnel—nurses, physicians, aides, etc.—routinely seek and routinely record disclosures of patients. Such a practice will have a double benefit. Not only will it ensure that crucial information is noted and reported; it will also do much to vitiate the well-founded complaint of many patients that they are impersonally treated by health-profession personnel. Thus, it will strike positively at one source of the latent hostility which the lay public holds for medicine and nursing.

14

To Whom Can a Nurse Give
Personalized Care? *

It has become customary in most professions to classify
practitioners into various specialties, and the nonspe-
cialist is regarded as a "general practitioner" of his profession. In nursing, one speaks of nursing educators,
nursing supervisors, psychiatric nurses, obstetrical nurses,
medical-surgical nurses, and the like. These are convenient labels describing the place where the given nurse
works and the broad categories into which her clients—
patients, students, or other nurses—may be assigned. In
spite of their convenience, I believe that these classifica-
tion labels encourage a kind of unhelpful confusion in
thinking, teaching, and practice. We tend to think that
there is something special and basically different about
psychiatric nursing, or OB nursing, or pediatric nursing,
and I would like to propose that any differences are su-
perficial, and they mask something basic which all
branches of nursing share.

The "something basic" which is common to all phases
of nursing, and for that matter, to all helping professions, is the dedication of oneself to helping the other
fellow achieve worth-while objectives—health, comfort,
freedom from pain and suffering, the dissipation of ignorance, etc. Anyone who wants to be a helper needs
good will and a certain basic skill. This skill has been
called "interpersonal competence" (Foote and Cottrell,
1955). Interpersonal competence means the ability to
produce desirable and valued outcomes to one's transactions with people.

In the practice of caring for patients, interpersonal
competence is of course necessary. Nurses who have
achieved this kind of competence are able to achieve

* Presented at the annual convention of the National Student
Nurses' Association, Miami Beach, Florida, April 29, 1960.

desirable outcomes to their transactions with patients, and *their patients therefore must show signs of the quality of care that has been given*. What does a well-nursed patient look like, and how does he differ from one who has not been well-nursed? I am afraid that in the welter of studies published in professional nursing journals, not many have focused on the patient as the yardstick or gauge of nursing competence. Perhaps that will be the next stage in nursing research—to devise measures of patients' behavior, inner experience, and physical status that will correlate with measures of nurses' behavior, training and personality.

Let us pretend that we have already solved the problem of defining, describing, and measuring a well-nursed patient. We can assume he is as comfortable as his condition permits, he knows why he became ill and what is being done for him, he feels his nurses really care what happens to him, he knows *that they know him as a unique person* because they took the trouble to learn about him, and he knows he told them much about himself. He feels free to call for help when he wants it, and does so. His nurse "tunes in" on him at regular intervals, to sample his private, personal, psychological world as it were—not with an empty question, "How do we feel" —and she uses this information as the basis of actions which make him say "ah-h-h!" He wants to get well, and to get back into the community, and if his place in the community is one which imposes a lot of sickness-producing stress on him, the nurse has found this out and conveyed the information to a social worker, or the physician, or somebody who might be able to help improve the situation.

Who is this nurse who has been able to display such competence? And what are the characteristics of the patient which permitted the nurse to produce just those wonderful outcomes? At this point, I want to introduce a different concept of specialists and general practitioners in nursing. A specialist in nursing, according to this different view, is someone who can feel an identity with and become concerned about the needs and wants of only a very small class of patients. An extreme case of a nursing specialist would be a nurse who could establish contact with and provide personalized care for only girls aged 20 from her neighborhood in Palatka. Everyone else is a threat, a mystery, an object of distrust, disgust, or indifference to her. These other people—and they include everyone else in the world but 20-year-old girls from her neighborhood in Palatka—are treated as objects, as categories, as things, but not as people. The extreme specialist of this sort may have the identical number of nonpersonal nursing skills as a general nursing expert has, but she can apply them in the context of a person-to-person contact, producing optimum outcomes only with this very narrow range of patients. Patients outside the restricted range are a puzzle or a threat to her, and *she doesn't want to get to know them.* She takes care of their bodies, but not their whole selves.

Let us play awhile with this idea of nursing specialists. Remember, we are talking here about nurses who have received standard minimum training, so that they can do all the technical things that nurses are expected to be able to do. But we are also talking about the ability to produce in a patient the feeling of being understood, because he is understood; the feeling that his nurse cares for and about him because she does; the feeling of comfort that follows care above the call of duty, whatever that means. Any nurse can stick a needle or an enema into anything human, and for that matter, into beings which are not human. But not all nurses can supply optimum care as we have outlined it to all patients.

Now, to illustrate. There are nurses who cannot care for patients who are known to be immoral. One of our students mentioned that with some young mothers of illegitimate children who were having their babies in a local hospital, she would stay a minimum length of time and get out of the room as fast as she could. We can call this girl a goodness specialist.

There are white nurses who cannot care for Negro patients. Let us call these nurses "white specialists."

There are nurses who are repelled by sex and who balk at taking care of patients who make passes. We might call these specialists "nurses of neuters."

There are nurses who cannot take care of people whose behavior is at first bizarre and incomprehensible, as is sometimes true of so-called psychiatric patients. We might call these nurses "normality specialists."

There are nurses who can do what is called for only with patients unconscious on the operating table. A conscious patient induces anxiety, threat, bashfulness, etc. We might call these nurses "coma specialists."

There are nurses who can care only for Protestants. Catholics, Jews, Hindus, agnostics, and Zen Buddhists arouse their anxiety and indignation, and they provide only minimum care for people in these categories. We might call these nurses "Protestant specialists."

I think that by now you have grasped the meaning I intend with this different concept of specialist. Simply stated, these specialists are nurses who can provide personalized, warm, responsive care, prompted by spontaneous concern, for only a small segment of humanity. Everyone outside the segment only gets impersonal care —strangers doing things to strangers.

What, then, is a general nursing practitioner? This is an ideal that is never achieved by any particular nurse, but it is useful as a goal toward which to aim. A general nursing practitioner is a person who is able to get into empathic contact with anybody who is sick, whether white or Negro, young or old, Protestant or Catholic, moral or immoral. If she cannot immediately understand this very patient, she strives to learn his language, his view of the world, his values, his wants, so that she can then care for him. She cares about *people*, not just one narrow segment of the population, and she wants to know them, help them, and be an effective agent in their recovery toward comfort and wellness.

Who is this paragon? A better question is, who has the greatest chances of becoming such a growing paragon who broadens her range of competence with each person nursed? The becoming general nursing practitioner is a person who is open to her own experience, who genuinely cares about people and about herself. This is important. She cares about herself. The proof of effective caring about oneself is a self which is happy, growing, open. A person who cares about himself has been cared for in the past and is being cared about in the present by others. This person is free then to care about others.

This paragon is a person who is always in process of maturing and growing. What I mean by this is she can look into her own memory and experience and find that she has suffered, thought, felt, wished, and enjoyed just about everything human beings anywhere under the sun have experienced. This openness to herself makes it possible for her to establish empathic contact with the patients as they come and go. She realizes that each patient is unique, and that *there is no automatic, easy way to take care of individual patients*—only of people who fall into a category and who have thus lost all vestiges of individuality. Consequently, she never assumes that she knows a patient before she has taken steps to become acquainted and re-acquainted with the reality of his self, his inner experience.

Every one is a specialist of one sort or another. But this is a fact of life, not a condemnation. Nobody but God is a full-fledged general practitioner of nursing—that is, able to love everyone in the active sense (though some people seem to think that God loves only the people in their club).

The more that you experience as a person, inside a sick-room and in outside life, the more progress you make toward general practice. The more suffering, enjoying, sinning, being afraid, becoming psychotic and recovering, being sick, reading books, having babies, fighting and arguing, loving and making up, daydreaming—in short, living and learning about yourself—the more you move toward general practice.

Now what I just said can be stated another way. The more you grow as a person, the less shocked you become about people who are different from yourself. And in many ways, the more you grow, the more different and the more similar you become to everyone. I say similar because with living comes the feelings, hopes, fears, doubts, joys, and sorrows that all humans share because they are human. I say different because every single person is a variation on the human theme and commands respect for his difference.

Actually, there is something about training that can actively obstruct growth toward general practice. This is the view that practice makes perfect and that repeated practice makes for effortlessness. We live in what I call the "Fat Society"; we worship the idol called ease. Now there is point in becoming efficient and even unconscious in the performance of standard skills, like injections, bed-making, and so on, because the speed and effectiveness frees time for other pursuits. But let me push the cult of effortless nursing to its logical extreme. Let us pretend that, through scientific busy-work, we could construct an automatized hospital. I will outline what it would be like.

Each patient lies in his own cubicle, and there is attached to him all kinds of wires, connected to his brain, his muscles, his viscera. Every time these wires, which are actually electronic pick-ups, transmit signals to a computer indicating that a bladder is too full, a bowel stuffed, the patient hungry or in pain, before you could blink an eye, the computer sends signals to different kinds of apparatus which empty the bladder and bowel, fill the stomach, scratch the itch, massage the back, and so on. We could even mount each bed on a slowly moving belt; the patient gets in a bed at one end, and four or six days later his bed reaches the exit, and the patient is healed—we hope. Certainly a dream (or nightmare) factory of this sort would solve the technical problems and the leg-work problems which many nurses either complain about or delegate to auxiliary personnel. But what would the nurses do with their time then? And what would the patients be like?

About the only thing that such machines cannot provide is human warmth, love, and responsive care. Do patients need this? Or do they merely need sanitary surroundings, medicine, and rest?

Let me suggest to you that patients get sick, not only because germs and viruses infect them, but rather because their bodies, at one time fairly sterile environments for cancer cells, bacteria, and viruses, suddenly become very fertile, as if fertilized, and the alien cells and germs grow like weeds. When does this happen? Recent research findings (Schmale, 1958; Wolff, 1953) strongly suggest that illness begins when a person's life begins to lose zest, a sense of future, meaning, and love. When one's relationships with people become impersonal, a stage of vague depression or a drop in spirits takes place, the person loses hope, and sickness will begin unless there is a change in the way the person sees the situation. There is growing reason to suspect that people become well, not alone because of the medicines they take, but because of the meaning the medicines have for the patient. The patient has faith in medicine, doctors, and all the symbols and rituals of the modern hospital. If the patient has faith neither in doctors nor in hospitals, he will likely fail and die. There is a lot of ground for suspecting that most healing is faith healing —the patient has faith in the healing rituals. (See Chapters 9, 10, and 11.)

One of the events which we believe inspires faith and hope in patients is the conviction that somebody cares about him. If this proves true, it implies that the quality of the nurse-patient relationship is a factor in the patients' recovery. Direct contact with a patient somehow increases his sense of being a worth-while individual person, and this experience inspirits him—it does something to the body which helps it throw off illness.

Sincere attempts to know and to understand a patient, and to help him be comfortable, increase his sense of identity and integrity, and this experience seems to be a factor in healing.

On the other hand, contempt, indifference, insincerity, and impersonal relationships with patients undermine their sense of self and identity and make them feel like nobodies. Perhaps some nurses are experts at making all patients feel like nobodies by "treating them all alike," like robots or piles of meat.

It seems to me that "personal nursing" is something that machines cannot do; but it also seems to me that nurses, in their efforts to make their practice of care efficient, impersonal, and effortless, are actually competing with machines, and becoming machine-like in the process. Even the most impersonal of nurses, however, become human when they are called on to treat some patient who falls within the range of their specialty— the splinter of humanity which they regard as human. Hopefully, nursing practitioners will soon learn that nursing is just a special case of loving. You can't love somebody you don't know, and you can't love someone you don't respect. Knowing patients calls for inquiry. Respect for patients' individuality calls for maturity, for growing acquaintance with one's own inner experience, so that one can find something like the patient in one's own experience. General nursing calls for the ability to see that which is common to all mankind in oneself and in the other person. This means that to know all mankind, one begins by looking within oneself.

15

Roles That Sicken and Transactions That Heal *

There is growing reason to suspect that hope, purpose, meaning, and direction in life produce and maintain wellness, even in the face of stress, whereas demoralization by the events and conditions of daily existence helps people become ill. Schmale (1958) found, for example, that 41 out of 42 patients admitted to a general hospital during a 23-day period showed evidence in interview of feelings of helplessness or hopelessness shortly before the onset of their variegated diseases. This loss of morale was typically associated with a disruption in the relationship of the patient with a significant other. Schmale reported that such feelings of helplessness or hopelessness may actually set the stage for illness to occur when it does.

In a different study, Canter (1960) was able to discriminate suicidal from nonsuicidal psychiatric patients, and between each of these groups and a group of normals, on the basis of scores derived from the Minnesotal Multiphasic Personality Inventory. The questionnaire items on which the scores were based had reference primarily to diminished self-esteem, and Canter called his scale a measure of Morale Loss. Scores on the Morale Loss Scale further differentiated between fast and slow recovery from brucellosis, and between subjects with histories of frequent medical illness and those with little illness in their backgrounds.

Both these studies represent attempts scientifically to verify impressions long held by laymen and later by physicians, nurses, and psychologists that one's attitude toward life and self are factors both in the onset of ill-

* Presented at the meeting of the Alabama Nurses' Association, Montgomery, Alabama, November, 1960, and published in the *Canadian Nurse Journal*, July, 1961.

ness and in the recovery therefrom. These two studies
can serve nicely therefore as a point of departure for a
discussion of a revolution which is going on in current
thinking about wellness and disease, a revolution that
has profound implications for practitioners in the healing professions. Clearly it *must* have such implications,
since the theory of disease and health that is extant during a given epoch more or less serves as a guide to both
prevention and rehabilitation.

Schmale's and Canter's studies suggest that if we want
to find psychological factors that predispose toward lowered resistance to illness, that foster reduced effectiveness
in living, we should look into transactions and events in
everyday life that produce a sense of hopelessness, such
as a loss of the sense of identity and self-esteem, loneli-
ness-producing events or ways of life, or more generally,
what I call *dispiriting* events. Let me propose as a general definition that events, relationships, or transactions
which give a person a sense of identity, of worth, of hope
and of purpose in existence are "inspiriting," while those
that make a person feel unimportant, worthless, hopeless, low in self-esteem, isolated, frustrated, which make
him feel that existence is absurd and meaningless, are
"dispiriting." The hypothesis is that dispiriting events
render an organism vulnerable to the always present
forces of illness, of entropy, of disintegration, while inspiriting events mobilize the forces of wellness latent in
all organisms.

Sickness, whether mental or physical, seems to be one
of several ways (cf. Parsons, 1951) in which people express protest against a way of life that will not support
wellness. People become ill, not just because of germs,
viruses, trauma, or stress, but because these assaults fall
upon receptive hosts. Hinkle (1959) has adduced evidence to show that the so-called "normal" ways of life
most of us live are interrupted by sickness about 10 times
a year, the sickness including headaches, colds, flu, diarrhea or constipation, or more serious ailments. Something about the normal or usual way of life must periodi-
cally dispirit average people, if they become ill with such
regularity. Let us explore normality and seek to identify

those aspects of being an average person which dispirit and hence permit illness to arise.

Organisms have self-regulating, homeostatic mechanisms built into them such that when balance is disrupted, signals are emitted, and these elicit reflex and behavioral compensatory responses that restore dynamic equilibrium. At the human level, many of these signs of disruption (I call them "all is not well" signals) reach conscious awareness. They are capable of being discriminated and are identifiable as pain, depression, boredom, frustration, anxiety, or just generalized malaise. By and large, these signals will first arise in weak intensity as a person pursues his customary round of everyday activity, and hence are usually ignored. They are most likely to be ignored when they are of low intensity, or if they arise more intensely, in people who are unable to notice what is going on inside of them. In our culture we are trained from an early age not to pay too much attention to our inner selves, to our own feelings, wishes, and needs, but are instead urged to listen to the commands of others or to the promptings of conscience. This has been described by Murray, Adorno, and others as anti-intraception. By the time most of us reach adulthood, we have lost intimate contact with our actual selves. Indeed, we only know that our real needs and feelings are being ignored when we begin to feel uexplained anxiety, or boredom, or irritation, or a sense of emptiness in our existence. But we seldom know *why* we feel these things. As a matter of fact, pressures to play our various roles in the "proper" way actually foster increased self-alienation. If we have been taught to believe that only certain kinds of wishes, feelings, and thoughts should go on inside us, then if we look inside and find other, horrendous wishes and feelings that life has induced in us, we actively turn away from ourselves in horror.

Now, when "all is not well" signals are thus ignored, the person goes on doing whatever it was that he was doing that produced the low-level discomfort signals, instead of giving pause and seeking to change his conduct to do better justice to his needs. If the person's everyday activity authentically is no good for the integrity of his total personality, then the assault on his wellness continues inexorably. Consequently, even more intense signals will eventually arise. The person will then become so full of pain, or boredom, or anxiety, that he cannot continue his customary round of behavior, the very round which was sickening him. When he thus stops his usual work and play, when he temporarily resigns his normal role-obligations as parent, spouse, worker, friend, or playmate, we say he is sick. He may then say, "I can't carry on as usual because I am now sick." It might be closer to the facts if he said, *"I am sick because I carried on as usual."* Of course, it is also true that abrupt changes in roles, relationships, surroundings or ways of life that had previously sustained wellness will dispirit people and thereby promote illness (cf. Wolff, 1953, pp. 10-35). But I suspect that gradual dispiritation is more common and less noticeable *because* of its gradualness.

The *usual* round of activity gradually dispirited the person, resulting in lowered resistance to infection, lowered ability to rebound from the effects of stresses, and lowered ability to suppress the primitive psychological reactions latent in all of us, which, when manifest, we call mental illness. In my opinion, *it is this felt necessity to play roles in a standard, procrustean manner, withholding and suppressing the while our own spontaneous and idiosyncratic selves, which gradually dispirits us and makes our bodies fertile gardens for disease of any and all kinds.*

When people feel compelled to suppress their identities in order to seem respectable to themselves as well as to others (consciences are villains here; see Horney, 1950, pp. 64-85), important consequences follow. First to be mentioned is a loss of sensitive awareness of one's inner experience. We already have indicated how this can permit low-level signals of incipient illness to be ignored. Another outcome of such suppression and repression of spontaneous inner experience is that added stresses are imposed on organisms already burdened with the normal stresses of everyday life. I say this because it consumes energy to suppress behavior, and when people are wearing masks, as they do, dreading to be known, then *other* people become chronic sources of threat and stress to them. Then too, when people are obliged to play the role of spouse, friend, child, or worker in some *stereo-typed* way, the while withholding their inner selves from the gaze of others, it inevitably follows that other people will never really come to know them. Remaining unknown may be a relief, but it has its price. How can anyone know you unless you make yourself known to them through full and free disclosure? And how can anyone meet your needs, for example, if you will not make them known, because of fear of criticism or because of guilt? How, for that matter, can you know your own needs if you have become estranged from your real self? And if you do not know what you really want or need in order to find satisfaction and meaning in life, it follows that neither your behavior nor that of another loving or well-intentioned person will ever truly "hit the spot." In short, rigid enactment of roles must inevitably produce both unwanted loneliness—the feeling of not being known or understood (Van Kaam, 1959)—and gradual dispiritation following the failure of behavior to bring rewards. There; I believe I have just finished describing what might be called the "normal" personality of our time. He is "normal" just in the sense of being typical, not normal in the sense of manifesting joyous and abundant health utilized to pursue a meaningful, purposeful, satisfying existence.

Students of animal behavior have shown that when an animal, such as a rat, is trained to press a lever at a certain rate in return for periodic rewards of food, he will keep on responding so long as there remains hope of reward. Even the animal will stop, however, when the boring activity of lever-pressing fails to pay off in rich satisfaction. So it is with people. There are many parallels to hopelessly unrewarding lever-pressing in a rat among humans—for example, drudgery and lack of challenge in work, nagging loneliness and emptiness in personal life, and rigid, impersonal roles which destroy identity and spontaneity in everyday dealings with family or friends. We learn a repertoire of roles and behavior patterns called "personality" and perform this repertoire in our everyday lives, not because it satisfies our needs, but rather because it is safe or socially acceptable. If this repertoire fails to do justice to our assorted wishes and needs, then inevitably we will become lonely, bored, hopeless, or depressed—in short, dispirited—and in this condition we seem to be more prone to illness resulting from the stresses and pathogens that are always with us (Wolff, 1953).

The real question should not be, "Why do people get sick?" Rather, we should ask, "Why aren't people sick all the time?" I think we would find that those people who seldom become sick are people who have found ways of life that permit them to be and to express their selves, ways which yield purpose, meaning, hope, interest, and reasonably rich satisfactions of needs for affection, love, sex, status, and achievement, and yet they are reasonably respectable in their conduct. The healthier people, when they find their present ways of life dull, frustrating, or tedious, pay attention to their "all is not well" signals *and change what they are doing, including their ways of behaving with others*. But this is the joker. It is difficult and anxiety-provoking to change what one is doing, to change one's way of interacting with others; powerful forces from within and without tend to restrain change, and so most of us keep up the way of life that has been slowly "doing us in." Therefore, we become sick, and it is usually with some measure of surprise. It is still an unsolved question why the sickness is "physical" for some and "psychiatric" for others. I am coming to suspect that those who are often physically ill are people who commit "altruistic suicide" (cf. Durkheim, 1951, pp. 219-221) by slow degrees. They are slowly destroying their bodies, as it were, for the preservation of their roles and the social systems in which they regularly participate. They are victims of their sense of duty. The psychiatrically ill seem to resemble rebels without courage or effectiveness.

Being sick is a temporary respite from the dispiriting conditions of our existence up to the onset of the illness. Incidentally, if it seems to a patient that his usual life, the one that made him sick, cannot be changed, he may never get well. Why should he? Or if he does recover but then resumes his usual life, he'll be sick again before long. As he leaves the hospital, we could safely say, and mean it, "Hurry back." If illness has not proceeded too far, when we get sick we merely get into our own beds. If sickness has proceeded to a point where it seems the body or mind cannot restore itself unaided, we then take to the hospital, and let the experts have at us.

At the point where people have become sick, I want to make a digression. Medicine has made much progress in describing and labeling the various syndromes of illness; much progress has even been made in identifying the proximate causes of these syndromes, and devising pharmacological or surgical methods for neutralizing them. But, it is estimated that except for perhaps 15 per cent of all illnesses, rest or change alone will permit the organism to restore itself to the premorbid level of functioning. Official medicine and the media of mass communication have not sufficiently publicized the healing powers of changed conduct, changed surroundings, and rest, and seem to place more faith in the healing powers of drugs. I have yet to turn on my television set and hear the announcer say, "What do doctors recommend? In a recent survey, three out of four doctors recommended fishing, or golf, or love, as remedies for nagging backache, headache, etc." Who would sponsor such announcements anyway? People have been so brainwashed that they will hardly feel they have been treated *unless* some medicines have been prescribed and ingested, or unless they have been cut open. In spite of efforts to minimize the so-called placebo effect in drugs and other therapeutic measures, it has not been possible to state with scientific confidence that medicines heal people. When the evidence is assessed impartially, it seems likely that the patients' *faith* in the healing powers of the doctor, his rituals, his medicines, and his aseptic temples is the true medicine. How else can we account for the many authentic instances of gravely ill people responding to prayer, to proximity to shrines, to chiropractic, to Christian Science, to the mumbo jumbo of voodoo witch-doctors, and to sweet, pink pills, and any other symbols of healing power in which he may place his faith? We need to devote our best scientific talent to intensive investigation of the psychophysiological mechanisms which are brought into play when sick people have their faith and confidence inspired by supposed healing symbols and rituals. Actually, we know that healing is rooted in the biological structure of the organism, not in drugs, surgery, or manipulations. We need to identify what might loosely be called the "healing reflexes," part of which are doubtless psychological, and determine what conditions will bring them under the control either of a therapist or of the sick person himself. If we had a program devoted to the identification of the factors in the so-called placebo effect, to understanding of the relation of faith to healing, just as we did in the case of the development of polio vaccine, we might learn much that is new about illness and recovery therefrom.

Actually, the failure of health-scientists to devote their truth-yielding research efforts to the study of how placebos, Christian Science, chiropractic, and the symbols of medical know-how all promote healing is a fantastic oversight, attributable to what I do not know, unless it is to the *zeitgeist* or to the subtle brainwashing effects of propaganda from drug companies. Physicians since time immemorial have noticed that placebos have healing effects (Shapiro, 1960). Rather than investigate them rigorously, they have used them, but shamefacedly, viewing the patients who respond to them as stupid, suggestible, or not really sick. Research indicates that the physiological effect of drugs or surgery accounts only for *part* of the total variance in healing and that perhaps a greater proportion, maybe all, can be accounted for by the attitude toward, and faith in, treatment manifested by or inspired in the patient.

If it is true that performance of roles that dispirit contributes to the onset of illness in patients, and if it is true that the gratification of needs, being known and cared for, being identified and treated as oneself, and being permitted to be oneself are factors in the attainment of wellness, then nurses in hospitals have a job carved out for them. How can they relate to patients so that the latter will feel known, will feel free to be themselves, so that they will feel they are *not* being treated just like everyone else? If inspiriting events foster healing and full functioning, how can nurses learn to relate to patients in ways that "inspirit" them? Most professions have emphasized the importance of "good interpersonal relationships," but careful study shows that what so-called interpersonal experts among nurses actually do is institute clever manipulations which make the patient do what he is supposed to do. In short, much of contemporary interpersonal competence seems to entail suaveness in getting patients to conform to the roles they are supposed to play in the social system of the hospital so that the system will work smoothly, work will get done faster, and the patients will be less of a bother to care for. It would seem that there has been a movement afoot in the nursing professions to train practitioners to teach patients how to become good "organization men" whose behavior will be good for the organization of a ward, but not necessarily good for the attainment of identity, or even of wellness. Psychology has promulgated techniques like operant conditioning, propaganda, hypnosis, smiling, and other cold-blooded methods for inducing liking or obedience, to a wide array of vested interests— to advertisers, politicians, administrators, and educators as well as to nurses.

There is something self-defeating about the practice of treating people who have become ill, in part because of rigid, demoralizing role requirements, by casting them in equally rigid role requirements—those inherent in the patient role. My anthropologist colleague, Carolyn Dickinson-Taylor (1960), writes in this connection,

> . . . (There is) a peculiarly 20th Century expedient of adjustment—the *stripping technique* . . . (which) reduces the individual to an interchangeable unit. These mass interchangeable units are then labelled in terms of their function: average student, consumer, patient, doctor, nurse, etc.
>
> The first step in the process of stripping is removal of the old frame of reference (or identity) . . . which is accomplished by means of administrative procedure. In the case of the patient, the procedure is called "admissions" . . . for the doctor or nurse, it is called medical school or nurses' training.

Mrs. Taylor concludes her paper with the observation that not only patients, but also doctors and nurses, have been subjected to sociological sheep-shearing, to a shearing of their identities, which has made them over from

persons into interchangeable parts. Patient care and cure
must suffer, she says, in direct proportion to the effectiveness with which training and administrative procedures
have stripped people, changing them from human persons
into doctors, nurses, and patients. I might add that the
wellness of doctors and nurses is jeopardized when they
play their roles with chronic impersonality.

Recently, one of my colleagues at the College of Nursing gave a report in a conference on an "obnoxious"
patient. This woman was able to make her peculiarities
known to almost every doctor in town and to all the
staff of our own hospital. She was demanding, she insisted on endless reassurance, she didn't like the way
she had been treated. In short, she was generally regarded
as a "crock" and as a pain in the neck. There was general
agreement among the nurses that this woman was obnoxious, and many suggestions were made concerning
how she should be treated. These ran the gamut from
having her referred to psychiatry for shock treatment—
an excellent way to trim the rough edges and the identity
from a person—to various slick suggestions as to how she
could be made more reasonable.

Now I will agree that people in the raw, people who
don't play the game the way that they should, are "difficult" for most of us. But does this mean that we should
only attempt to help those people who "deserve it" because of their "good behavior"?

Somehow, if nursing is to rise to its potential status in
the healing arts, nurses must grow to the point where
they become able to establish communicative contact
with a broad range of people, because it would seem that
such contact is a *sine qua non* for helpful nursing transactions. I am coming to believe that it is the peculiar
privilege of nurses to play, not just an important role in
healing, but possibly *the* important role. Nurses are potentially (when they don't run from the bedside into
impersonal administration) with patients more than
doctors or even relatives. If they can permit patients to
be themselves in their presences and not be driven away
by whatever the patients bring forth when they are thus
granted freedom of self-expression; if they can communicate profoundly with patients, so that the latter overcome

a profound sense of loneliness that seems to be part of illness—an outcome if not a cause; if they can help patients feel that here is someone who cares, to whom their feelings and wishes matter, they may so restore identity and morale to patients that they get well in spite of the usually impersonal regimen of hospital life.

If "inspiriting" events foster healing, and if close communicative relationships with patients are inspiriting, then it follows that every transaction in which a nurse has established contact with a patient so that he knows she knows what is on his mind will foster healing. If acknowledgment of requests, however bizarre, immature, or spoiled they may show the patient to be, is inspiriting, then it follows that every time a nurse hears a request, takes it seriously, tries to understand it, and does her best to meet it will foster healing. Automatic bedside manners, stereotyped ways of playing the nurse role, which then thrust the patient back into the dispiriting anonymity of the patient role, cannot be inspiriting. Somehow, nurses, who can be crucial healers, must learn to *create* their roles (Smith, 1960), guided by cues provided by the peculiarities of each patient; there is no evidence to suggest that the role-definition of nurse acquired in school,* or as described in the "line-item" budget, will necessarily be healing for the patient (or healthy for the nurse). Perhaps the most general and vague, yet accurate, way of proposing how nurses can be more effective healing agents or catalysts is for them to struggle to establish personal contact with this very patient, who, like most of us, may feel condemned to solitary confinement in the prison of his own skin and his own role.

I think that nurses will better learn the art of role-creation, a new role with each patient, when two things take place. The first is a change in hospital structure such that nurses' roles are not so tightly defined by job descriptions of administrators. Rather, nurses should be freed from many of the chores which serve mainly to keep the wheels of administration functioning smoothly.

---

* I think we need to add an Americanized version of *geisha* training to the nursing curriculum in order to graduate more nurses who inspirit more patients. It's too bad that this suggestion is not likely to be taken up by nursing educators.

The second change must come from *within* any particular nurse. She must be able to profit from increased freedom "to be." In the University of Florida Teaching Hospital, many non-nursing functions have been assigned to clerks and unit managers and nursing assistants, thus freeing RN's for more personal contact with patients. It would be foolish to say that this hospital is without problems, but some progress has been made there in the direction of freeing nurses to establish the kind of personal contact which inspirits patients. Interestingly enough, the anthropologist employed there noted that the nurses, when their previous clerical tasks were taken away, reacted much like amputees with a hallucinated phantom limb. And so the anthropologist consulted with occupational and physical therapists, to find how they helped people who had lost a limb mobilize their resources and even emerge from the experience more fully functioning than they were when they had all their limbs. The insights gained thereby proved helpful in the rehabilitation of nurses *to nursing* following the "amputation" of such functions as laundry sorting, record keeping, and the like. Another factor which seems to help nurses become freer to establish the contact and the relationships which inspirit is a kind of inner freedom that comes from effective psychotherapy—the freedom and courage to be oneself. We have made some progress in this direction with our faculty through three years of in-service education meetings in which all participants have been encouraged and permitted to be and to disclose themselves on all manner of topics. The dividends in empathy, resourcefulness, and enhanced ability to establish contact with others have been considerable. Our faculty are excellent nurses as well as teachers and seem expert at inspiriting patients as well as students.

Let me conclude with a prophecy—that at some future time, more people will have learned to notice their "all is not well" signals and will have the courage to change their behavior *before* they have gotten sick. Those who *have* become sick may be treated less with drugs and surgery, and more with human relationships that heal.

16

Epilogue: The Invitation to Authenticity

This entire book can be regarded as an invitation to "authentic being." Authentic being means being oneself, honestly, in one's relations with his fellows. It means taking the first step at dropping pretense, defenses, and duplicity. It means an end to "playing it cool," an end to using one's behavior as a gambit designed to disarm the other fellow, to get him to reveal himself *before* you disclose yourself to him. This invitation is fraught with risk, indeed, it may inspire terror in some. Yet, the hypothesis of the book is to the effect that, while simple honesty with others (and thus to oneself) may yield scars, it is likely to be an effective preventive both of mental illness and of certain kinds of physical sickness. Honesty can literally be a health-insurance policy.

The invitation of which I speak is intended for everyone, but, being a psychologist, I extend it particularly to my colleagues, both in psychotherapy and in psychological research.

I have begun to think about psychotherapy, not as a quasi-medical treatment where interpretations are dispensed instead of pills or injections, but rather as an invitational process—perhaps even a temptation. It fascinates me to think of psychotherapy as a situation where the therapist, a "redeemed" or rehabilitated dissembler, invites his patient to try the manly rigors of the authentic way. The patient is most likely to accept the invitation, it has seemed to me, when the therapist is a role-model of uncontrived honesty. And when the therapist is authentically a man of good will, he comes to be seen as such, and the need for sneaky projective tests or for decoding hidden messages in utterances vanishes. The patient then wants to make himself known, and proceeds to do so. In this defenseless state, the interpretations, suggestions, and advice of the therapist then have maximum, growth-yielding impact on him.

This view of therapy, incidentally, brings it into an interesting relationship with other helping arts. Probably the most effective minister is one who knows sin, who knows the short-run pleasures and longer-run hell of sneaking, and who has learned how to find satisfaction and meaning in a more righteous life. Because he knows sin, he can address the sinner with empathy. But he won't get many to accept his invitation unless his very being as a man is in some ways living proof that one can be righteous without being joyless, priggish, or bored.

And let us look at the good teacher. Probably he can be seen, without too much strain, as a rehabilitated ignoramus. He has known the hellish smugness of the cliché, the quick answer, the unchallenged certitude; he has known the awe of mystery, and the dread of the unknown—and the adventure of the life of endless inquiry. Since his pupils are presently ignoramuses, he knows how to reach them. But they are not likely to accept the invitation to a life of inquiry unless by his very being as a man, the teacher is revealed as a man who has courage and who finds satisfaction and meaning, and even some money, in his life.

So, the good therapist need not have been psychotic or neurotic. These are, after all, only extreme outcomes of a long career as a phony. He need only have been expert at dissemblance, suffered from it, gone through the pangs of reawakened authenticity, and then add technical know-how to his repertoire of responses.

Now what about my colleagues in research? How curious it has seemed to me that our textbooks in psychology are written about man as an habitual *concealer* of himself. I am beginning to think that we, as researchers, have actually fostered self-concealment and inauthenticity in our human subjects, and then reported that human subjects are notoriously duplicitous. Our psychologies of perception, of learning, of motivation, of interpersonal relations have all grown out of research where the investigator has concealed his purposes from the subject, and the latter has likely been in a defensive, self-conscious mode of functioning. What would happen if we began an all-out program of replication, where we repeated all studies previously undertaken with human subjects, but with this change: we regarded the subject as a *collaborator*, and not as an unfortunate substitute for a pigeon, rat, or analogue computer. What would our findings be if we informed our subjects about ourselves, our purposes, our methods, our arguments with colleagues, etc. Perhaps the subjects would adopt a less defensive mode of functioning, and we might learn a great deal that is new. This seems to be the implication for psychological research of Buber's (1937), poetic dictum, "The *I* in the primary word *I-Thou* is a different *I* from that of the primary word *I-It*."

A Technical Appendix for Psychologists

AI

A Research Approach
to Self-Disclosure*

by Sidney M. Jourard and Paul Lasakow†

The present paper describes a questionnaire method for measuring the amount and content of self-disclosure to selected "target-persons," and reports the results of three exploratory studies. Self-disclosure refers to the process of making the self known to other persons; "target-persons" are persons to whom information about the self is communicated.

The process of self-disclosure has been studied by others from various points of view. Block (1) and Block and Bennett (2) have demonstrated that the content of communication about the self is a function of variations in "own-role." Lewin (7) noted differences between typical Germans and Americans regarding their readiness to confide personal information to others. Jourard (6) has suggested that accurate portrayal of the self to others is an identifying criterion of healthy personality, while neurosis is related to inability to know one's "real self" and to make it known to others. Characterological studies of Fromm (3), Riesman (9), and Horney (4) have called attention to a tendency common among persons in our society, to misrepresent the self to others. This tendency is central to the "marketing personality," the "other-directed character," and the "self-alienated" individual, as these have been described by their respective authors. Since much of social science is founded upon the self-disclosures of respondents, the conditions and dimensions

* Reprinted from the *Journal of Abnormal and Social Psychology*, Vol. 56, No. 1, January, 1958.
† The authors are indebted to Drs. A. J. Riopelle, Emory University, and O. Lacy, University of Alabama, for statistical advice.

of self-disclosure bear directly upon the validity of many purported facts in the social sciences.

From the foregoing, it may be concluded that systematic analysis of self-disclosure holds promise of yielding information that is relevant to diverse areas of theory and method.

The following questions were proposed for investigation:

1. Do subjects (Ss) vary in the extent to which they disclose themselves to different target persons, for example, mother, father, male friend, and female friend? What is the effect of the Ss' marital status on self-disclosure to parents and friends? What is the effect of the Ss' feelings and attitudes toward particular target-persons upon self-disclosure to them? The last question was investigated only with respect to the relationship between Ss' disclosure of self to parents, and their feelings and attitudes toward their parents.

2. Are there differences between categories of information about the self (aspects of self) with respect to self-disclosure? Do Ss tend to disclose some aspects of self more fully than others?

3. Are there differences ascertainable between Negro and white Ss with respect to self-disclosure?

4. Are there sex differences regarding self-disclosure?

INSTRUMENTS

The Self-Disclosure Questionnaire. A sixty-item questionnaire was devised. As can be seen in Table 1, the items are classified in groups of ten within each of six more general categories of information about the self (aspects). Ss were given the following instruction for completing the questionnaire:

The answer-sheet which you have been given has columns with the headings "Mother," "Father," "Male Friend," "Female Friend," and "Spouse." You are to read each item on the questionnaire, and then indicate on the answer-sheet the extent that you have talked about that item to each person; that is, the extent to which you have made yourself known to that person. Use the rating-scale

TABLE 1

The Self-Disclosure Questionnaire

Attitudes and Opinions

1. What I think and feel about religion; my personal religious views.
2. My personal opinions and feelings about other religious groups than my own, e.g., Protestants, Catholics, Jews, atheists.
3. My views on communism.
4. My views on the present government—the president, government, policies, etc.
5. My views on the question of racial integration in schools, transportation, etc.
6. My personal views on drinking.
7. My personal views on sexual morality—how I feel that I and others ought to behave in sexual matters.
8. My personal standards of beauty and attractiveness in women—what I consider to be attractive in a woman.
9. The things that I regard as desirable for a man to be—what I look for in a man.
10. My feeling about how parents ought to deal with children.

Tastes and Interests

1. My favorite foods, the ways I like food prepared, and my food dislikes.
2. My favorite beverages, and the ones I don't like.
3. My likes and dislikes in music.
4. My favorite reading matter.
5. The kinds of movies that I like to see best; the TV shows that are my favorites.
6. My tastes in clothing.
7. The style of house, and the kinds of furnishings that I like best.
8. The kind of party, or social gathering that I like best, and the kind that would bore me, or that I wouldn't enjoy.
9. My favorite ways of spending spare time, e.g., hunting, reading, cards, sports events, parties, dancing, etc.
10. What I would appreciate most for a present.

Work (or studies)

1. What I find to be the worst pressures and strains in my work.
2. What I find to be the most boring and unenjoyable aspects of my work.
3. What I enjoy most, and get the most satisfaction from in my present work.

(TABLE 1, *Continued*)

Work (or studies) (Continued)

4. What I feel are *my* shortcomings and handicaps that prevent me from working as I'd like to, or that prevent me from getting further ahead in my work.
5. What I feel are my special strong points and qualifications for my work.
6. How I feel that my work is appreciated by others (e.g., boss, fellow-workers, teacher, husband, etc.)
7. My ambitions and goals in my work.
8. My feelings about the salary or rewards that I get for my work.
9. How I feel about the choice of career that I have made—whether or not I'm satisfied with it.
10. How I really feel about the people that I work for, or work with.

Money

1. How much money I make at my work, or get as an allowance.
2. Whether or not I owe money; if so, *how much*.
3. Whom I owe money to at present; or whom I have borrowed from in the past.
4. Whether or not I have savings, and the amount.
5. Whether or not others owe me money; the amount, and who owes it to me.
6. Whether or not I gamble; if so, the way I gamble, and the extent of it.
7. All of my present sources of income—wages, fees, allowance, dividends, etc.
8. My total financial worth, including property, savings, bonds, insurance, etc.
9. My most pressing need for money right now, e.g., outstanding bills, some major purchase that is desired or needed.
10. How I budget my money—the proportion that goes to necessities, luxuries, etc.

Personality

1. The aspects of my personality that I dislike, worry about, that I regard as a handicap to me.
2. What feelings, if any, that I have trouble expressing or controlling.
3. The facts of my present sex life—including knowledge of how I get sexual gratification; any problems that I might have; with whom I have relations, if anybody.
4. Whether or not I feel that I am attractive to the opposite sex; my problems, if any, about getting favorable attention from the opposite sex.

Personality (Continued)

5. Things in the past or present that I feel ashamed and guilty about.
6. The kinds of things that make me just furious.
7. What it takes to get me feeling real depressed or blue.
8. What it takes to get me real worried, anxious, and afraid.
9. What it takes to hurt my feelings deeply.
10. The kinds of things that make me especially proud of myself, elated, full of self-esteem or self-respect.

Body

1. My feelings about the appearance of my face—things I don't like, and things that I might like about my face and head—nose, eyes, hair, teeth, etc.
2. How I wish I looked: my ideals for overall appearance.
3. My feelings about different parts of my body—legs, hips, waist, weight, chest or bust, etc.
4. Any problems and worries that I had with my appearance in the past.
5. Whether or not I now have any health problems—e.g., trouble with sleep, digestion, female complaints, heart condition, allergies, headaches, piles, etc.
6. Whether or not I have any long-range worries or concerns about my health, e.g., cancer, ulcers, heart trouble.
7. My past record of illness and treatment.
8. Whether or not I now make special effort to keep fit, healthy, and attractive, e.g., calisthenics, diet.
9. My present physical measurements, e.g., height, weight, waist, etc.
10. My feelings about my adequacy in sexual behavior—whether or not I feel able to perform adequately in sex-relationships.

that you see on the answer sheet to describe the extent that you have talked about each item.

The self-disclosure rating-scale was as follows:

0: Have told the other person nothing about this aspect of me.

1: Have talked in general terms about this item. The other person has only a general idea about this aspect of me.

2: Have talked in full and complete detail about this item to the other person. He knows me fully in this respect, and could describe me accurately.

X: Have lied or misrepresented myself to the other person so that he has a false picture of me.

The numerical entries were summed (X's were counted as zeros), yielding totals which constituted the self-disclosure scores.

Seventy white unmarried college students of both sexes were tested for self-disclosure to Mother, Father, Male Friend, and Female Friend, in a study of reliability. Since the questionnaire included 60 items, and there were four target-persons, a total of 240 entries were made by each S. These 240 entries were divided into halves by the odd-even method, and the subtotal sums were correlated with each other. The resultant r, corrected, was .94, indicating that the Ss were responding consistently to the questionnaire over all target persons, and all aspects of self.

Parent-Cathexis Questionnaires. Mother-cathexis and Father-cathexis questionnaires, fully described elsewhere (5), were employed to test Ss' feelings toward their parents. The Ss rated their feelings about 40 parental traits, e.g., *sense of humor, temper, ability to make decisions,* in accordance with the following scale:

1: Have strong positive feelings; like very much.
2: Have moderate positive feelings.
3: Have no feelings one way or the other.
4: Have moderate negative feelings.
5: Have strong negative feelings; dislike very much.

High scores indicated negative feelings toward the parents, while low scores signified positive feelings.

SUBJECTS

The Ss included in the studies to be reported were taken from larger samples drawn from three Alabama college populations: two white liberal arts colleges, a Negro liberal arts college, and a school of nursing located at a medical school. For the combined sample 300 white and Negro liberal arts college sophomores and juniors were obtained, and 55 white nursing students. All Ss were tested in groups by an examiner of the same race.

For the purpose of analysis, the following randomly

selected subsamples were drawn from the combined samples:

1. From the 300 liberal arts students, a subsample of 10 white males, 10 white females, 10 Negro males, and 10 Negro females was drawn for the study of differences in self-disclosure associated with race, sex, targets, and aspects of self. All Ss were unmarried, and, in all cases, the parents were living. Mean ages were: white males, 21.70, SD 2.00; white females, 20.30, SD .90; Negro males, 22.10, SD 2.02; and Negro females, 20.40, SD .45. All Ss had been tested for self-disclosure to Mother, Father, Male Friend, and Female Friend.

2. From all the white respondents in the combined sample, a subsample of 10 married male and 10 married female Ss was drawn for comparison with the first subsample of 10 unmarried males and 10 unmarried females to test the effects of marriage on self-disclosure patterns. These Ss had indicated self-disclosure to Mother, Father, Same-sex Friend, and Spouse. Mean age for the married males was 23.40, SD 1.43, and for the married females, 20.60, SD 2.42.

3. Thirty-one unmarried nursing students comprised the third sample, used to examine the relationship between parent-cathexis and self-disclosure to the parents. Mean age for this group was 18.59, SD 3.53.

The data were analyzed according to Lindquist's (8) Type VI model for analysis of variance with mixed "between-within" effects. Critical differences for t ratios at the .01 level were computed between all groups, targets, and aspects of self when F ratios proved significant. Pearsonian r's were computed between Mother-cathexis scores and scores for disclosure to the mother, and between Father-cathexis scores and the corresponding disclosure scores, within the group of 31 nursing students to whom these two instruments had been administered.

RESULTS

Influence of Race, Sex, Target-Differences, and Aspects of Self. Table 2 shows the results of analysis of variance of the self-disclosure scores of the 40 white and

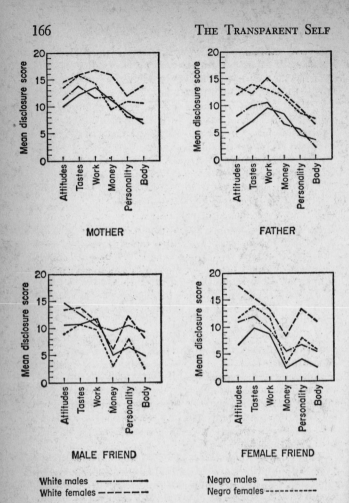

Fig. 1. *Mean Self-Disclosure of White and Negro, Male and Female Ss to Mother, Father, Male Friend, and Female Friend.*

TABLE 2

*Analysis of Variance of Self-Disclosure Scores of White and Negro,
Male and Female Subjects*

Source	Mean Square	df	Error Term	F
Between Groups	892.33	3	Error(b)	6.78†
Males vs. Females	573.50	1		4.36*
Whites vs. Negros	2076.82	1		15.78†
Sex × Race	126.67	1		
Error(b)	131.61	36		
Total df Between		39		
(Within-Groups Comparisons)				
Between Target-Persons	557.06	3	Error$_1$(w)	10.89†
Between Aspects of Self	952.01	5	Error$_2$(w)	40.39†
Target × Aspect	87.49	15	Error$_3$(w)	15.38†
Group × Target	128.11	9	Error$_1$(w)	2.50*
Group × Aspect	32.16	15	Error$_2$(w)	1.36
Group × Target × Aspect	9.61	45	Error$_3$(w)	1.69*
Total df Within		92		
Error$_1$(w)	51.17	108		
Error$_2$(w)	23.57	180		
Error$_3$(w)	5.69	540		
Total Error df		828		
Total df		959		

* $p < .05$.
† $p < .001$.

Negro Ss, while Fig. 1 portrays mean self-disclosure
scores classified by targets, groups, and aspects of self.
The findings may be summarized as follows:

1. The four groups differed in total self-disclosure.
Table 3 shows that the white Ss disclosed more than the
Negroes, and the females more than the males.

2. The combined group of 40 Ss varied in amount of
self-disclosure to different persons. They disclosed the
most to Mother, and in lesser amount to Father, Male
Friend, and Female Friend, as shown in Table 4. Sex-
and race-differences in disclosure to the four target-persons

TABLE 3

Differences Between Groups in Mean Disclosure Scores

Group	Mean*	SD	Differences†		
			Negro Males	White Females	Negro Females
White Males	248.50	68.60	+62.60	−45.10	+33.50
Negro Males	185.90	36.10		−107.70	−19.10
White Females	293.60	45.20			+78.60
Negro Females	215.00	57.60			

* Highest possible score, 480.

† Critical difference for $t = 2.72$, $p < .01$, $df = 36$ is 13.95 (cf. 8, p. 93). All differences are thus significant at $p < .01$.

is shown clearly in Fig. 1. Noteworthy is the consistently lower amounts of self-disclosure to Father on the part of Negro Ss.

3. The combined group of 40 Ss varied in self-disclosure according to aspects of self. Table 5 shows that two clusters of aspects appeared—a "high disclosure" cluster comprised of Tastes and Interests, Attitudes and Opinions, and Work, and a "low disclosure" cluster that included Money, Personality, and Body.

TABLE 4

Differences Between Targets in Mean Disclosure Scores

Group	Mean*	SD	Differences†		
			Father	Male Friend	Female Friend
Mother	72.30	19.50	+20.60‡	+17.12‡	+16.72‡
Father	51.70	24.13		−3.48	−4.88‡
Male Friend	55.18	22.43			1.40
Female Friend	56.58	27.70			

* Highest possible score, 120.

† Critical difference for $t = 2.63$, $p < .01$, $df = 108$ is 4.21 (cf. 8, p. 93).

‡ $p < .01$.

TABLE 5

Differences in Mean Disclosure Scores Classified by Aspects of Self‡

| | | | Differences† | | | | |
Aspect	Mean	SD	Tastes	Work	Money	Pers.	Body
Att.	45.35	14.20	−4.93‡	−2.30	+13.12‡	+11.30‡	+19.15‡
Tastes	50.28	13.98		+2.63	+18.05‡	+16.23‡	+24.08‡
Work	47.65	13.65			+15.42‡	+13.60‡	+21.45‡
Money	32.23	15.65				−1.82	+6.03‡
Pers.	34.05	13.45					+7.85
Body‡	26.20	14.28					

* Highest possible score, 80.
† Critical Difference for $t = 2.63$, $p < .01$, $df = 180$, is 2.87 (cf. 8, p. 93).
‡ $p < .01$.

4. There was significant interaction between targets and aspects, groups and targets, and groups, targets, and aspects. The group-by-aspect interaction was not significant.

Influence of Marriage. Separate analyses of variance compared married with unmarried males, and married with unmarried females. The results are shown in Table 6, for males, and Table 7, for females. In the analyses, Opposite-sex Friend and Spouse were treated as equivalent target-persons.

No differences were found between married and unmarried Ss in total amount of self-disclosure. Figs. 2 and 3 show, however, that: (a) married Ss disclosed less to the parents and the same-sex friend than unmarried Ss, and (b) there was more disclosure to the Spouse than to any other target-person by married or unmarried Ss.

Marriage thus appears to have the effect, not of increasing or decreasing the total extent to which Ss disclose themselves, but of producing a redistribution of self-disclosure. The married Ss "concentrated" self-disclosure upon the spouse, and became more reticent toward other persons. In this sense, self-disclosure enters into relations similar to those of libido in psychoanalytic theory.

Parent-Cathexis and Self-Disclosure to Parents. Total Mother-Cathexis scores for the group of 31 nursing students correlated −.63 with scores for self-disclosure to Mother; Father-Cathexis scores correlated −.53 with

TABLE 6

Analysis of Variance of Self-Disclosure Scores of Married and Unmarried Males

Source	Mean Square	df	Error Term	F
Between Groups	37.95	1	Error(b)	.17
Error(b)	228.81	18		
Total df Between		19		
(Within-Groups Comparisons)				
Between Target-Persons	232.99	3	$Error_1(w)$	6.10*
Between Aspects of Self	477.49	5	$Error_2(w)$	24.80†
Target × Aspect	21.72	15	$Error_3(w)$	4.19†
Group × Target	676.95	3	$Error_1(w)$	17.72†
Group × Aspect	1.00	5	$Error_2(w)$	.00
Group × Target × Aspect	22.24	15	$Error_3(w)$	4.49†
Total df Within		46		
$Error_1(w)$	38.21	54		
$Error_2(w)$	19.25	90		
$Error_3(w)$	4.95	270		
Total Error df		414		
Total df		479		

* $p < .01$.
† $p < .001$.

scores for self-disclosure to Father. Both coefficients were significant beyond the .01 level for $df = 29$. The direction of the obtained values signifies that high self-disclosure was associated with positive feelings toward the parents, while low self-disclosure was associated with attitudes of dislike toward the parents.

DISCUSSION

These preliminary findings demonstrate that self-disclosure is measurable, and that the present method for assessing it has some validity. The questions now open for exploration are virtually without limit, in view of the many possible and relevant combinations of the main factors—groups, target-persons, aspects of self, and individual differences.

Some questions suggested by the present findings may

TABLE 7

Analysis of Variance of Self-Disclosure Scores of Married and Unmarried Females

Source	Mean Square	df	Error Term	F
Between Groups	186.25	1	Error(b)	1.38
Error(b)	135.27	18		
Total df Between		19		
(Within-Groups Comparisons)				
Between Target-Persons	349.90	3	Error$_1$(w)	6.08*
Between Aspects of Self	345.54	5	Error$_2$(w)	18.91†
Target × Aspect	46.64	15	Error$_3$(w)	8.00†
Group × Target	531.48	3	Error$_1$(w)	9.23†
Group × Aspect	15.63	5	Error$_2$(w)	.86
Group × Target × Aspect	26.01	15	Error$_3$(w)	4.46†
Total df Within		46		
Error$_1$(w)	57.56	54		
Error$_2$(w)	18.27	90		
Error$_3$(w)	5.83	270		
Total Error df		414		
Total df		479		

* $p < .01$.
† $p < .001$.

serve as guides to further exploration: Why do Negro Ss consistently disclose less about themselves than whites, and why do females disclose more than males? Why is the mother the preferred target of self-disclosure for this age group? What is the significance of the fact that some aspects of self, for instance, Tastes and Interests, Attitudes and Opinions, and Work, are disclosed more than information about Personality, Money, and Body? Is it an artifact of the questionnaire, or does it reflect cultural consensus about what is readily disclosable and what is not? What individual traits besides feelings and attitudes toward target-persons account for individual differences in self-disclosure?

SUMMARY

A reliable questionnaire for the assessment of self-disclosure was described. Groups of both sexes, white and

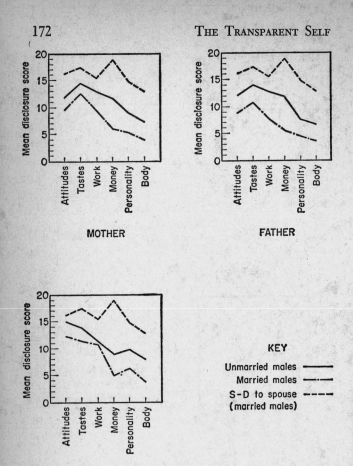

Fig. 2. *Comparison of Married and Unmarried Males on Self-Disclosure to Mother, Father, and Male Friend. (The curve for disclosure to Spouse is shown in each panel.)*

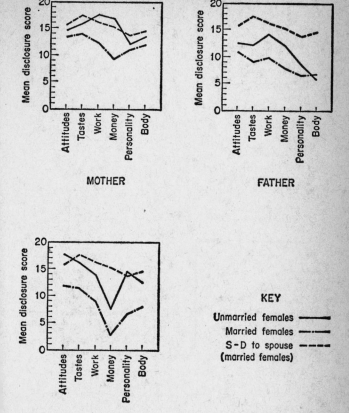

Fig. 3. *Comparison of Married and Unmarried Females on Self-Disclosure to Mother, Father, and Female Friend. (The curve for disclosure to Spouse is shown in each panel.)*

Negro, married and unmarried, were tested with the
questionnaire for extent of self-disclosure of six different
aspects of self to various target-persons—Mother, Father,
Male Friend, Female Friend and/or Spouse. The findings
are summarized as follows:

1. Young unmarried Ss, both white and Negro, showed
the highest self-disclosure to Mother, with lesser amounts
to Father, Male Friend, and Female Friend.

2. Ss tended to vary the amount of self-disclosure with
respect to the category of information to which an item
about the self belonged. Two clusters of aspects emerged,
a high disclosure cluster including Attitudes and Opinions, Tastes and Interests, and Work, and a low disclosure cluster comprised of Money, Personality, and Body.

3. White Ss disclosed more than Negroes, and females
more than males.

4. There was significant interaction among groups of
Ss, target-persons, and aspects of self.

5. Married Ss disclosed less to Mother, Father, and
Same-sex Friend than comparable unmarried Ss. The
married Ss disclosed more to their Spouses than to any
other target-persons. There was more disclosure to
Spouses than to any other target-person on the part of
the married and the unmarried groups.

6. A significant correlation was found between parent-
cathexis and self-disclosure to the parents. The more the
parents were liked, the more disclosures were made to
them.

REFERENCES

1. BLOCK, J. The assessment of communication. Role variations
     as a function of interactional context. *J. Pers.*, 1952, 21,
     272-286.
2. BLOCK, J., AND BENNETT, LILLIAN. The assessment of com-
     munication. Perception and transmission as a function of
     the social situation. *Hum. Relat.*, 1955, 8, 317-325.
3. FROMM, E. *Man for himself.* New York: Rinehart, 1947.
4. HORNEY, KAREN. *Neurosis and human growth.* New York:
     Norton, 1950.
5. JOURARD, S. M. Identification, parent-cathexis, and self-
     esteem. *J. consult. Psychol.*, 1957, 21, 375.
6. JOURARD, S. M. *Personal adjustment: An approach through*

the study of healthy personality. New York: Macmillan, 1958, in press.

7. LEWIN, K. Some social-psychological differences between the United States and Germany. In G. Lewin (Ed.), *Resolving social conflicts: Selected papers on group dynamics, 1935-1946.* New York: Harper, 1948.

8. LINDQUIST, E. F. *Design and analysis of experiments in psychology and education.* Boston: Houghton Mifflin, 1953.

9. RIESMAN, D. *The lonely crowd.* New Haven: Yale Univer. Press, 1950.

A2

Some Findings in the Study of Self-Disclosure

Whenever one constructs a measuring tool, one wonders whether it is reliable and whether it actually measures what it is supposed to measure. We have been able to demonstrate that our questionnaires (of lengths that include 15, 25, 35, 45, and 60 items) have satisfactory reliability (odd-even coefficients for larger subtotals run in the 80's and 90's), and results until now show this method has some validity. It should not be overlooked, however, that there are always fundamental flaws in any personality measure that is based on self-report. With this precaution in mind, let me proceed to narrate some of our findings.

SUBJECT-MATTER DIFFERENCES

We found that certain categories of personal data are consistently disclosed more fully by our subjects to various target-persons than to others. For example, information bearing upon one's work, one's tastes, hobbies, and interests, one's attitudes toward religion, politics, and the like are evidently more disclosable than the details about one's sex life, one's financial status, and one's feelings and problems in relation to one's body and to one's own personality (Jourard and Lasakow, 1958). There are evidently strong social norms at work here, norms that even extend across the Atlantic, for we found (Jourard, 1961) that female college students in England show patterns of disclosure and concealment of subject matter that are almost identical with those found among American coeds. Melikian (1962), at Beirut, Lebanon, has shown similarly consistent patterns in Near Eastern samples. Male and female Puerto Rican college students likewise resemble Americans in their differential disclosure of subject matter (Jourard, 1963).

Anyone who has conducted psychotherapy knows that patients will more readily disclose some kinds of personal data and will block, or show resistance, with respect to others. Such resistance has been demonstrated with polygraphic measures taken on patients during therapeutic interviews—for example, Davis and Malmo's (1951) work with electromyograms and Dittes' with the GSR (1959). I have shown, by means of what I called my "wiggle-chair" (a stratolounger chair equipped with a movement transducer) that subjects will show increases in their base-rate of movement when they are asked to disclose some kinds of personal data by a given interviewer; and different interviewers elicit different outputs of wiggle, no matter what the subject matter. Of course, there are interactions among interviewee, subject matter and interviewer operative here. Our questionnaire measures also yielded significant interaction between subject matter and target-persons, which signifies only that it makes a difference to whom one discloses what.

TARGET-DIFFERENCES

All our questionnaire studies have shown significant differences in the total amount of personal data that Ss have disclosed to the various target-persons that we included for consideration, viz.: parents, closest friends, and spouse. As you might expect, the spouse is typically the one to whom most is disclosed. Indeed, the amount of mutual disclosure spouses engage in exceeds the amount that unmarried people disclose to *anyone*, whether parent, relative, or friend (cf. Jourard and Lasakow, 1958). This confirms the view that marriage is the "closest" relationship one can enter, and it may help us the better to understand why some people avoid it like the plague. Anyone who is reluctant to be known by another person and to know another person—sexually and cognitively— will find the prospective intimacy of marriage somewhat terrifying.

Among unmarried subjects, we find a complex pattern of target-preferences that is related to the age of the

subjects. Female college students in their late teens indicate that they disclose in about comparable degree to
their mothers and closest girl-friends, while they keep
their fathers and their present boy-friends somewhat
more in the dark. Male college students of similar age
keep their parents about equally informed about their
subjective being, and in lesser degree, than do females.
The person who knows these boys best is their closest
male friend. Their female friend is typically disclosed
less authentic and varied personal information than is
their chum. I must mention the consistency with which
we found that the father is disclosed to in the least degree by our subjects. Father is evidently kept more in
the dark about the subjective side of his children than
are other people. He is the last to know what is going
on. This is a finding of interest to sociologists and psychiatrists alike! We may conclude from findings like
these that the role of the target-person *vis-à-vis* the self
is an important determiner of disclosing oneself to him.

   When we focused more directly upon a given target-
person in a fixed social role, such as parent, or friend,
we found some further correlates of the amount of disclosure. The degree of liking for a target-person was
found to correlate substantially with the amount disclosed to him—but, interestingly enough, more strikingly
among women than among men. We found that women
show this correlation between liking and disclosure to
mother, father, and work-associates (Jourard and Lasakow, 1958; Jourard, 1959); among men, the comparable
correlations were markedly lower (Jourard and Landsman, 1960). This finding strongly suggests that women
are more responsive to their own feelings—that is, they
vary their interpersonal behavior in accord with their
feelings more so than men do. Both sexes show a correlation between the degree to which they *know* a given
target-person and their disclosure to him. Men, evidently, trust their brains, their cognition of the other person more than their feelings, as a condition for self-
disclosure.

   Related to degree of knowing is another interesting,
and I think fundamentally important, datum: for males
and females alike, a very strong correlate of disclosure

output to a given target-person was the amount of disclosure *input* from that person. I called this input-output correlation the *dyadic effect* (Jourard, 1959; Jourard and Landsman, 1960), and I have proven in my own practice that it extends to the realm of psychotherapy. I have suggested further that the capacity to disclose authentically, *in response* that is appropriate to the setting, to the authentic disclosure of the other person in a dyad is probably one of the best indicants of healthy personality. It betokens, to use Buber's (1957) terms, the capacity to enter into and sustain dialogue. I think that overly-technical psychotherapists as well as novices probably fall down on the ability to give an authentic, self-revealing response to the disclosures of their patients, and block, thereby, the ongoing process of the therapeutic dialogue. In Buber's terms, they have the capacity for "distance," but not for "entering into relation." Probably, they are still painfully self-conscious about their techniques, and the therapeutic dyad for them is a secret triad—the supervisor is psychically more present to the novice than is the patient. Likely, too, they have little faith or trust either in the healing powers of their own real selves or in the good will of their patients who would come to know them.

GROUP-DIFFERENCES

In this context, I will report some of the over-all differences between groups that we found with our questionnaire measures. You must keep in mind that we were measuring the amount disclosed by an individual to four target-persons. Since there was always interaction between group and target-person, the possibility exists that total disclosure scores based on the sum for all four target-persons may not be different, and yet there could be significant differences between groups in the amount disclosed to a *given* target-person. The findings I wish to report now were ones in which the difference in disclosure output was general—that is, it extended across target-persons.

The most consistent difference we found was between the sexes, with women indicating that they disclosed

more about themselves than men (cf. Jourard and Lasakow, 1958; Jourard and Landsman, 1960). I must qualify
this finding by saying that it has not been without exception in my studies, and at least two investigators in
the northeast failed to find a sex difference at all. Thus,
Rickers-Ovsiankina and Kusmin (1958) at Connecticut
and Zief (1962), at Harvard did not find the women
to be higher disclosers than the men. In fact, Rickers-
Ovsiankina found her college male subjects to be slightly
more "socially accessible" than women. It is tempting
to suggest that in the southeast, where I collected the
bulk of my data, the men are men and the women are
women; whereas Harvard males and Radcliffe females,
whom Zief tested, for example, may not be so different
from one another. More generally, the magnitude of the
sex-difference in disclosure-output between different
groups may be an illuminating phenomenon to study in
its own right. I have some data which show that the size
of the sex-difference varies in a non-chance way among
groups who differed in their performance on the Min-
nesota Multiphasic Personality Inventory, for example.

In the realm of national differences, we found (Jourard, 1961c) that English co-eds were consistently lower
disclosers to the significant people in their lives than
comparable American females. Melikian (1962) did not
find differences between nine different Far Eastern samples in *total* disclosure output, but did find a significant
group by target interaction. He did not report his target
means, a serious oversight, so we do not know on which
target persons his various populations differed in disclosure output. However, I compared the mean total disclosure scores he reported with scores obtained by male
college students tested with a questionnaire identical
with his, and the American mean totals were substantially higher. No test for the significance of the difference was possible.

I have some recent data (Jourard, 1963) showing
comparisons between N's of 25 male and 25 female
Puerto Rican college students with the same N's of
American college students, matched for age, religion
(mostly Catholic), and fathers' occupational level. The
Puerto Ricans had significantly lower total disclosure

scores than the Americans. Among the males, the differences extended across all four target persons. In the female sample, the Americans disclosed more to Father, opposite-sex friend, and same-sex friend, but less to Mother than did the Puerto Rican girls. It may well be true that Americans talk more about themselves to others than just about any other cultural group.

A study of interdenominational differences showed that Catholic, Methodist, and Baptist college males did not differ significantly from one another in disclosure output, but they all disclosed less, on the average, than Jewish male college students. Among the females, these denominations did not differ among one another, suggesting that their sex-role was a stronger determiner of their self-disclosing behavior than their religious affiliation (Jourard, 1961b). One wonders at the greater openness of the Jewish males in comparison with their non-Jewish fellow students. Perhaps it betokens a greater need or capacity for intimate personal relationships than is typical for the American culture at large.

I collected data (unpublished) which showed that applicants for clinical services at the campus psychological counseling center were lower disclosers than matched groups of students who had not sought such services. The main trend approached significance, but it tended to be obscured by the fact that some of the applicants for counseling obtained unusually *high* disclosure scores, especially to their parents, in comparison with controls. This suggests that excessive disclosure may be as incompatible with optimum adjustment in the college milieu as unduly low disclosure. Parenthetically, I may add that in one study I cited above (Jourard, 1959), the two women least liked by their colleagues were, respectively, the highest and lowest disclosers of self in their work setting.

Here is a finding that may interest those who are concerned with gerontology. We found (Jourard, 1961a) that, as people get older, the amount they disclose to other people in their lives, especially parents and same-sex friend, gradually diminishes. Disclosure to opposite-sex friend, or spouse, increases from the age of 17 up to about the fifties and then drops off. It is possible that, with increased age, the communicative intimacy of relationships with others diminishes, possibly an illustration of the disengagement phenomenon that Henry and Cummings (1959) have written about.

Another group difference that warrants mention has to do with rated interpersonal competence. We tested nursing students with a disclosure questionnaire (Jourard, 1962). A year later, at the end of their period of clinical practice, they were rated for ability to establish and maintain a communicative relationship with patients. The students who received the highest ratings were significantly higher disclosers on the test they had taken the year before than the students receiving the lower ratings. It would appear that those who were most accustomed to making their own subjective being accessible to others learned the most readily to elicit the subjective being of others.

Again with nursing students, we found substantial correlations between scores for disclosure to mother and to girl-friend (obtained while the girls were sophomores) and accumulated grade-point average in *nursing* courses at time of graduation. The students were graded, in nursing courses, not only for knowing correct answers on objective quizzes, but also for ability to convey to their instructors the meaning of their experience at working with patients, reading assorted books and papers, etc., in so-called reaction papers and on essay examinations. Evidently those students least able to be open with female target-persons were least able to behave in the open way with the nursing faculty, the way which seemed to facilitate learning and performance of the valued sort. Two years later, I repeated this study, with a different self-disclosure questionnaire, and got comparable results, though the correlations were not so high.

Here is a group difference which is of a different sort, but one fraught with implications, I believe. Powell (1962) tested a group of underachieving college students at the University of Florida with a self-disclosure questionnaire and with a test of personal security. We anticipated that the underachievers would be lower disclosers and more insecure people than a matched group of adequately achieving students. There were no differences between these groups in mean disclosure to any target-person, and there was some slight evidence that achieving males (but not females) were more independently secure than underachieving subjects. Then, we turned up a nice nugget. Among the achieving males and females, significant correlations were found between closeness to peers and personal security; the comparable r's among underachievers were not significant. Among underachievers, significant r's were found between disclosure to each parent and personal security. Such was not the case among the achievers. We interpreted these findings to mean that underachieving students were less mature, in the sense of being less emancipated from parents, than were achieving students. In other words, security among the underachievers was a function of the intimacy of the relationship with the parents, while security in the achieving groups was more independent of the vicissitudes of the parent-child relationship. Some further evidence that the correlation between self-disclosure scores and measures of intraindividual traits betoken dependency is provided by some data obtained by Terence Cooke (1962), who did a doctoral dissertation with me. He devised a measure of "manifest religious behavior" for Protestants. This questionnaire gets at the intensity of religious involvement by asking Ss to indicate the frequency with which they attend church, the amount of donation, frequency of prayer, etc. Cooke found insignificant r's between measures of disclosure to parents and strength of manifest religious behavior in a sample of 111 male college students between the ages of 17 and 22. I re-analyzed his data, this time computing separate correlations between disclosure to mother and father and religious behavior for 17-18 year-olds, 19 year-olds, 20 year-olds, and 21-22 year-olds. I found that there were significant r's for the first two age levels, but not for the latter two. This finding indicates that religiosity is related to the degree of closeness to parents among late teen-agers, but becomes more independent of the parent-child relationship as the child becomes older. The utilization of the correlation between an interpersonal measure (self-disclosure scores) and an intrapersonal measure as an indicator of an underlying construct has intriguing methodological implications, it seems to me. It may, for example, point to a dimension of interpersonal "influencability" that is present in one group but not in another. The construct might then be approached more directly by other measurement procedures.

Let me now direct some final remarks about connections I see between self-disclosure as a mode of being with others, health, and psychotherapy.

SELF-DISCLOSURE AND HEALTH

Largely as a consequence of the writings of existentialist, Zen-Buddhist, and humanist philosophers and medical scientists, we are in the midst of a revolution in our thinking about man and his health. Inauthentic being is coming to be seen as an etiologic factor in mental illness, and there are even indications that susceptibility to physical illness is related to inauthentic being. What do existential writers mean when they speak of inauthenticity? What do Zen authors refer to with terms such as "the dual mode"? In my opinion, they are referring to the tendency to treat oneself as an object, a tool to be manipulated in ways thought necessary to bring about popularity, vocational success, power, and similar goals. When one treats oneself as a tool or as a thing, one treats others in the same way. This objectifying of the self is accompanied by *self-concealment*, or the repression of one's being and experiencing. This, in turn, results in what has been called self-alienation. A self-alienated person, among other things, does not know what he needs to sustain the wellness of his organism. He is desensitized to his experiencing, and hence will not recognize early warning signals that all is not well. It is as if he notices signals of danger to his job, car, or reputation, but does not sense the, at first, weak signals emitted by his organism that it is being badly used! Hence, his instrumental and interpersonal behavior must fail to gratify basic needs. Such privation is both stressing and dispiriting—and we have much indication that dispiritation or loss of morale diminishes resistance to infectious illness and impedes the process of recovery from illness. Now, to be open, or transparent to others, seems to be a necessary condition for being open to oneself. Knowing oneself and being known by another appear to be correlated. To the extent that vivid cognition of one's own experiencing is a factor in behavior that sustains wellness, and to the extent that knowing oneself and being known are correlated, we can see intimations of a complex relationship between self-disclosure and health.

One psychologist who has become even more outspoken than I am on the connection between self-disclosure and mental health is Hobart Mowrer (1961). He is convinced that the mentally ill—neurotic and psychotic—have developed their array of symptoms, at least in part, because of a duplicitous way of life. For Mowrer, therapy is seen as the confession of one's misdeeds and omissions to significant others, together with efforts at atonement or restitution.

I agree with much of Mowrer's view, and indeed, I feel that it can be extended to many who become physically ill. Perhaps honesty really is the best policy, in this case, a health-insurance policy.

SELF-DISCLOSURE AND PSYCHOTHERAPY

Increasing numbers of psychiatrists and psychologists are coming to see psychotherapy, not as something which one does to or for a patient, a treatment that calls for careful techniques of verbal responding, but rather as an exploration of the possibilities for dialogue between these two people. The patient may be viewed as one who is terrified of his spontaneous being and is initially unable to reveal himself freely in the therapeutic transaction. The therapist, in turn, may be afraid for many reasons to let himself respond in honesty to the patient. As time proceeds, the pair become increasingly able to carry out unself-conscious dialogue, so that the patient has no doubts in his mind concerning the subjective being of his therapist when the two are together; and the therapist likewise is clearly informed of the patient's experiencing as it unfolds. By this time, many of the symptoms will have vanished.

This concept of therapy is not congenial to many workers, who see it as a dangerous occasion for therapists to "act out" in ways that do no one any good. The technique-oriented therapist seems to expect his patient to be transparent to him, while he remains an enigma and a mystery, hiding his true experiencing behind a professional façade or couch-side demeanor. In another context, I have commented at length upon withholding of authentic disclosure in therapists, and I used the term "resistance in the therapist" to describe such a phenomenon. I think such chronic suppression of being in the therapist makes him sick!

The unduly technique-oriented psychotherapist may be proven to be least effective at helping his patients overcome impasses in their existence, for several related reasons. First of all, the behavior of a technical therapist is easily predicted by his patients, which, in turn, permits them to pick and choose their utterances and expression for some intended effect. Second, we know from research that people will disclose themselves most freely and fully to listeners who are *perceived* as being of authentic good will and as being honestly themselves rather than playing some contrived role. If a therapist is authentically *not* of good will, if he is faking his interest or feelings (instead, he is actually interested in proving his theories, or in making money, etc.), then in time he will be found out by his patient. Finally, the authentic responding of a therapist who has integrated his techniques with the rest of his person provides the patient with some social reality not usually accessible to him from more obviously technical therapists. This exposure to one's impact on another is very educational, to say the least. It maximally exposes one to the possibilities of social reinforcement, as one researcher at Duke (Gergen, 1962) has shown. He coined the term "reflective reinforcement" to describe the fact that honest responses from an interviewer reflect the interviewer's subjective being, and such responses can be effective at modifying a patient's self-concept. Gerald Goodman (1962), a researcher from Chicago, provided some further evidence of the therapeutic power of authenticity; he showed that, with experienced therapists, emotional self-disclosure of the patient and of the therapist increased as therapy progressed—a sort of dyadic effect.

We may conclude from all these data, and my tentative inferences from them, that self-disclosure is a measurable facet of man's being and his behavior, and that understanding of its conditions and correlates will enrich our understanding of man in wellness and in disease.

A3

Possible Points of Departure for Research in Spirit

1. Collect, by advertisement in medical and nursing journals, critical incidents which describe unusual experiences with placebos and descriptions of well-nigh miraculous recovery from imminent death. Search for common factors.

2. Review literature on studies of morale, of "suggestion," of faith and faith-healing.

3. Study people who live productive, loving lives.

4. Set up experimental hospital wards devoted to probing the limits of healing through mobilization of spirit, to discovering what patients have most faith in. Learn graduated dosages thereof; take regular physiological and biochemical measures to discern effects.

5. Study "inspiring" teachers and physicians and nurses. The problem of locating these: suggest peer-nominations, and nominations by students and patients.

6. Study psychogenic death.

7. Identify the Joe and Jane "Btflsks" (contemporary witches) in our society, study them and their impact on others, how they go about demoralizing and dispiriting others.

8. Try to localize, even roughly, the brain site of the neurophysiological counterpart of faith, *joie-de-vivre*, enthusiasm, etc.

9. Find a moderately sick patient who has faith in blood transfusion. Connect him to EEG, EMG, EKG, PGR, make blood-samples at minute intervals, tape-record his introspective free-association account—but give *no* transfusion, although he believes life- and health-giving fluids are gradually being infused into a vein. Maybe the correlated data would point to some central locus of faith.

10. Study the habits and commitments of aged peo-

ple at old-age homes and seek relationships between in-spirited commitments and death-age. Set up experimental group of people rated as dispirited and strive to in-spirit them; also compare their death rate with a control group.

11. Train nurses more effectively to discover means of inspiriting—e.g., "personalized" *geisha* nursing—and compare recovery rates and other pertinent measures with those taken from impersonally nursed patients.

12. Try, through conditioning, hypnosis, or high-prestige suggestion, to convince a population of the effectiveness of some given drug, odor, ritual, etc. See if it is possible to identify the responses which this "substance" affects. Perhaps pattern analysis of the peripheral effects of the substance may point to the more central loci of faith and the spirit-responses.

Bibliography

ALEXANDER, F., *Psychosomatic Medicine*. New York, Norton, 1950.

ALLPORT, G., *Becoming*. New Haven, Yale Univ. Press, 1955.

ANONYMOUS, A new theory of schizophrenia. *J. abn. soc. Psychol.*, 1958, 57, 226-236.

BARR, S., *Purely Academic*, New York, Simon & Schuster, 1958.

BORGATTA, E., The new principle of psychotherapy. *J. clin. Psychol.*, 1959, 15, 330-334.

BUBER, M., *I and Thou*, New York, Scribners, 1937.

BUBER, M., Elements of the interhuman. William Alanson White Memorial Lectures. *Psychiatry*, 1957, 20, 95-129.

CAMERON, N., AND MAGARET, ANN, *Behavior Pathology*. Boston, Houghton Mifflin, 1951.

CANTER, A. The efficacy of a short form of the MMPI to evaluate depression and morale loss. *J. consult. Psychol.*, 1960, 24, 14-17.

CHRISTENSON, W. N., KANE, F. D., WOLFF, H. G., AND HINKLE, L. E. Jr., Studies in human ecology: Perceptions of life experiences as a determinant of the occurrence of illness. *Clin. Res.*, 1958, 6, 238.

COMBS, A., AND SNYGG, D., *Individual Behavior* (2nd ed.), New York, Harper, 1959.

COOKE, T. F. Interpersonal correlates of religious behavior. Unpublished Doctor's Dissertation, University of Florida, 1962.

DAVIS, F. H., AND MALMO, R. B. Electromyographic recording during interview. *Amer. J. Psychiat.*, 1951, 107, 908-916.

DICKINSON-TAYLOR, CAROL. Sociological Sheep-Shearing. Unpublished Ms., College of Nursing, University of Florida, 1960.

DITTES, J. E. Extinction during psychotherapy of GSR accompanying "embarrassing" statements. *J. abn. soc. Psychol.*, 1957, 54, 187-191.

DOLLARD, J., AND MILLER, N. E. *Personality and Psychotherapy*, New York, McGraw-Hill, 1950.

DUNN, H., What high level wellness means. *Can. J. Public Health*, 1959(a), 50, 447-457.

DUNN, H. L. High-level wellness for man and society. *Amer. J. Pub. Health*, 1959(b), 49, 786-792.

DURKHEIM, E. *Suicide*. Glencoe, Free Press, 1951.

ENGEL, G. L. Studies of ulcerative colitis. V. Psychological aspects and their implications for treatment. *Amer. J. Digest. Dis.*, 1958, 3, 315-337.

EYSENCK, H. J. The effects of psychotherapy: an evaluation. *J. consult. Psychol.*, 1952, 16, 319-324.

FIEDLER, F. E., A comparison of therapeutic relationships in psychoanalytic non-directive, and Adlerian therapy. *J. consult. Psychol.*, 1950, 14, 436-445.

FIEDLER, F. E. A note on leadership theory: The effect of social barriers between leaders and followers. *Sociometry*, 1957, 20, 87-94.

FISHER, S., AND CLEVELAND, S. E. *Body-Image and Personality*. Princeton: Van Nostrand, 1958.

FOOTE, N. N., AND COTTRELL, L. S. *Identity and Interpersonal Competence*. Chicago: Univ. of Chicago Press, 1955.

FRANK, J. D., *Persuasion and Healing*, Baltimore: Johns Hopkins Univ. Press, 1961.

FRANKL, V. E., *The Doctor and the Soul, An Introduction to Logotherapy*. New York, Knopf, 1955.

FRANKL, V. E., *From Death Camp to Existentialism*. Boston, Beacon, Press, 1959.

FREUD, S. *The Interpretation of Dreams*. New York: Basic Books, 1955.

FROMM, E. *Man for Himself*. New York, Rinehart, 1947.

FROMM, E. *The Sane Society*. New York, Rinehart, 1955.

FROMM, E. *The Art of Loving*. New York, Harper, 1956.

GERGEN, K., Social reinforcement of self-presentation behavior. Unpublished Ph.D. Dissertation, Duke Univ., 1962.

GOODMAN, G. E., Emotional self-disclosure in psychotherapy. Unpublished Ph.D. Dissertation, Univ. of Chicago, 1962.

GREENSPOON, J. The reinforcing effect of two spoken sounds on the frequency of two responses. *Amer. J. Psychol.*, 1955, 68, 409-416.

GRODDECK, G., *The Book of It*. New York, Nerv. Ment. Dis. Pub. Co., 1928.

HALEY, J. The art of psychoanalysis. *ETC: a review of general semantics*, 1958.

HARTMAN, R. S., Value theory as a formal system. *Kant-Studien*, 1958/59, Band 50, 287-315.

HEIDER, F., *The Psychology of Interpersonal Relations*. New York, Wiley, 1958.

HENRY, W. E., AND CUMMING, ELAINE, Personality development in adulthood and old age. *J. proj. Tech.*, 1959, 23, 383-390.

HINKLE, L. E., On the assessment of the ability of the individual to adapt to his social environment, and the relation of this to "health" and "high-level wellness." (Unpublished report presented to subcommittee for the Quantification of Wellness. National Office of Vital Statistics, Washington, D.C., 1959.)

HINKLE, L. E., AND WOLFF, H. G., Ecologic investigations of the relationship between illness, life experiences and the social environment. *Ann. Int. Med.*, 1958, 49, 1373-1388.

HORA, T., The process of existential psychotherapy. *Psychiat. Quart.* 1960, 34, 495-504.

HORNEY, K. *The Neurotic Personality of Our Time.* New York, Norton, 1936.

HORNEY, K., *Neurosis and Human Growth.* New York, Norton, 1950.

HUXLEY, A., *Brave New World.* Garden City, New York, Sun Dial Press, 1932.

JAHODA, MARIE. *Current Concepts of Positive Mental Health.* New York, Basic Books, 1958.

JOURARD, S. M., *Personal Adjustment. An approach through the study of healthy personality.* New York, Macmillan, 1958 (2nd ed., 1963).

JOURARD, S. M., Self-disclosure and other cathexis. *J. abn. soc. Psychol.*, 1959, 59, 428-431.

JOURARD, S. M., Age and self-disclosure. *Merrill-Palmer Quart. Beh. Dev.* 1961(a), 7, 191-197.

JOURARD, S. M., Religious denomination and self-disclosure. *Psychol. Rep.*, 1961(b), 8, 446.

JOURARD, S. M., Self-disclosure patterns in British and American college females. *J. soc. Psychol.*, 1961(c), 54, 315-320.

JOURARD, S. M., Self-disclosure and grades in nursing college. *J. appl. Psychol.*, 1962.

JOURARD, S. M., Self-disclosure in the United States and Puerto Rico. (Unpublished data, 1963.)

JOURARD, S. M., AND LANDSMAN, M. J., Cognition, cathexis, and the "dyadic effect" in men's self-disclosing behavior. *Merrill-Palmer Quart. Behav. Dev.*, 1960, 6, 178-186.

JOURARD, S. M., and LASAKOW, P., Some factors in self-disclosure. *J. abn. soc. Psychol.*, 1958, 56, 91-98.

JOURARD, S. M., AND RICHMAN, P., Disclosure output and input in college students. *Merrill-Palmer Quart. Beh. Dev.*, 1963 9, 141-148.

JOURARD, S. M., AND SECORD, P. F., Body-cathexis and personality. *Brit. J. Psychol.*, 1955, 46, 130-138.

JUNG, C. G., *Modern Man in Search of a Soul.* New York, Harcourt Brace (Harvest Books), 1933.

KRASNER, L. Studies of the conditioning of verbal behavior. *Psychol. Bull.*, 1958, 55, 148-170.

LEARY, T., *Interpersonal Diagnosis of Personality*. New York, Ronald, 1957.

LEWIN, K. Some social-psychological differences between the United States and Germany. In Lewin, G. (ed.), *Resolving Social Conflicts: Selected papers on group dynamics, 1935-1946.* New York, Harper, 1948.

MASLOW, A. H., *Motivation and Personality*. New York, Harper, 1954.

MASLOW, A. H., *Toward a Psychology of Being*. Princeton, Van Nostrand, 1961.

MECHANIC, D., AND VOLKERT, E. H., Stress, illness behavior and the sick role. *Amer. Social Rev.*, 1961, 26, 51-58.

MELIKIAN, L. Self-disclosure among university students in the middle east. *J. soc. Psychol.*, 1962, 57, 259-263.

MILLER, J. G., Toward a general theory for the behavioral sciences. *Amer. Psychol.*, 1955, 10, 513-531.

MOLONEY, J. C., *The Magic Cloak. A contribution to the psychology of authoritarianism.* Wakefield, Mass., Montrose Press, 1949.

MOWRER, O. H., *The Crisis in Psychiatry and Religion.* Princeton, Van Nostrand, 1961.

MURPHY, G., *Personality, a Biosocial Approach to Origins and Structure.* New York, Harper, 1947.

PARSONS, T., Illness and the role of the physician: a sociological perspective. *Amer. J. Orthopsychiat.*, 1951, 21, 452-460.

PARSONS, T., AND BALES, R. F. *Family, Socialization, and Interaction Process.* Glencoe, Free Press, 1955.

POPPER, K. R., *The Open Society and Its Enemies.* Princeton, Princeton Univ. Press, 1950.

POTTER, S., *One-Upmanship; being some account of the activities and teaching of the Lifemanship Correspondence College of Oneupness and Gameslifemastery.* New York, Holt, 1952.

POWELL, W. J. Personal adjustment and academic achievement of college students. Unpublished Master's Thesis, Univ. of Florida, 1962.

REICH, W., *Character Analysis*. New York, Orgone Press, 1948.

REIK, T., *Listening with the Third Ear.* New York, Harcourt, Brace, 1949.

RICKERS-OVSIANKINA, MARIA, Social accessibility in three age groups. *Psychol. Reports*, 1956, 2, 283-294.

RICKERS-OVSIANKINA, MARIA, AND KUSMIN, A. A. Individual differences in social accessibility. *Psychol. Rep.*, 1958, 4, 391-406.

RIESMAN, D. *The Lonely Crowd.* New Haven, Yale Univ. Press, 1950.

ROETHLISBERGER, F. J., AND DICKSON, W. J., *Management and the Worker.* Cambridge, Harvard Univ. Press, 1939.

ROGERS, C. R. The concept of the fully functioning person (1954). In Rogers, C. R., *On Becoming a Person.* Boston, Houghton Mifflin, 1961.

ROGERS, C. R. The characteristics of a helping relationship. *Pers. Guid. J.,* 1958, 37, 6-16.

ROGERS, C. R. A theory of psychotherapy with schizophrenics and a proposal for its empirical investigation. In Dawson, J. G., Stone, H. K., and Dellis, N. P. *Psychotherapy with Schizophrenics.* Baton Rouge: Univ. of Louisiana Press, 1961.

ROGERS, C. R., AND DYMOND, R. F. *Psychotherapy and Personality Change.* Chicago, Univ. of Chicago Press, 1954.

ROSENTHAL, D., AND FRANK, J. D., Psychotherapy and the placebo effect. *Psychol. Bull.,* 1956, 53, 294-302.

RUESCH, J. *Disturbed Communication.* New York, Norton, 1957.

SCHMALE, A. H. Relation of separation and depression to disease. *Psychosom. Med.,* 1958, 20, 259-277.

SECORD, P. F., Facial features and inference processes in interpersonal perception. In Tagiuri, R., and Petrullo, L. (eds.), *Person Perception and Interpersonal Behavior.* Stanford, Stanford Univ. Press, 1958.

SELYE, H. *The Physiology and Pathology of Exposure to Stress.* Montreal, Acta, 1950.

SHAPIRO, A. K., A contribution to a history of the placebo effect. *Behav. Sci.,* 1960, 5, 109-135.

SHAW, F. J. Transitional experiences and psychological growth. *ETC: A review of general semantics,* 1957, 15, 39-45.

SKINNER, B. F. *Walden Two.* New York, Macmillan, 1948.

SKINNER, B. F. *Science and Human Behavior.* New York, Macmillan, 1953.

SKINNER, B. F. Teaching machines. *Science,* 1958, 128, 969-977.

SMITH, DOROTHY M. A nurse and a patient. *Nursing Outlook,* February, 1960.

SMITH, S., Self-disclosure behavior associated with two MMPI code types. M.A. Thesis, University of Alabama, 1958.

SOROKIN, P. The mysterious energy of love. *Main Currents,* September, 1958. Foundation for Integrated Education, Inc., New York.

STANDAL, S. W., AND CORSINI, R. J. (eds.) *Critical Incidents in Psychotherapy.* Englewood Cliffs, N.J., Prentice-Hall, 1959.

TILLICH, P., *The Courage to Be.* New Haven, Yale Univ. Press, 1952.

VAN KAAM, A. Phenomenal analysis: Exemplified by a study
of the experience of "really feeling understood." *J. individ.
Psychol.*, 1959, 15, 66-72.

WHITEHORN, J. C. The goals of psychotherapy. In Rubinstein,
E. A., and Parloff, M. B. (eds.) *Research in Psychotherapy.*
Washington, D.C., American Psychological Association, 1959.

WOLFF, H. G. *Stress and Disease.* Springfield, C. C. Thomas,
1953.

ZIEF, R. M. Values and self-disclosure. Unpublished Honors
Thesis, Harvard Univ., 1962.

Subject Index

Author Index